JUDY HALL

CRYSTAL HEALING

First published in Great Britain in 2005 by Godsfield, an imprint of
Octopus Publishing Group Ltd
Carmelite House
50 Victoria Embankment
London EC4Y 0DZ
www.octopusbooks.co.uk

An Hachette UK Company
www.hachette.co.uk

The authorized representative in the EEA is Hachette Ireland,
8 Castlecourt Centre, Dublin 15, D15 XTP3, Ireland (email: info@hbgi.ie)

This published in edition 2025

Distributed in the US by Hachette Book Group
1290 Avenue of the Americas, 4th and 5th Floors
New York, NY 10104

Distributed in Canada by Canadian Manda Group
664 Annette St., Toronto, Ontario, Canada M6S 2C8

ISBN 978-1-8418-1637-1

A CIP catalogue record for this book is available from the British Library.

Printed and bound in China.

10 9 8 7 6 5 4 3 2 1

Publisher: Lucy Pessell
Designer: Isobel Platt
Senior Editor: Tim Leng
Assistant Editor: Samina Rahman
Production Controllers: Lucy Carter and Nic Jones

MIX
Paper | Supporting responsible forestry
FSC® C104723

Disclaimer: The information in this book does not constitute medical advice, nor is it intended to take the place of medical treatment. A qualified crystal practitioner or medical doctor's opinion should be sought for all medical conditions.

JUDY HALL

CRYSTAL
HEALING

GODSFIELD

CONTENTS

INTRODUCTION

Crystals provide a gentle, non-invasive form of healing that co-operates with your body's inner healer, a repair mechanism that brings things back into balance or homeostasis. Working through vibration, resonance and colour, crystals heal holistically and dissolve dis-ease – that is to say, they act on your body, mind, psyche and spirit to restore equilibrium and rectify the underlying causes of a condition. Crystals are concerned with subtle electromagnetic energies and much of their work is done through realigning the biomagnetic sheath, or aura, that surrounds the physical body, and cleansing the chakras, the energy centres that link the two together.

While crystals work quickly for minor ailments, such as a headache, other conditions can take longer to heal. The habits of a lifetime and the ingrained attitudes that can underlie a disease, for instance, will not change overnight but with persistence crystals can transmute these to bring about a lasting improvement in your condition. However, healing does not necessarily imply a cure. Crystal healing takes into account the fact that your soul may be learning through your condition and, if this is so, the crystals will support you as you move through the process.

One of crystal healing's most profound effects is in helping you to uncover the psychosomatic causes of disease or dis-ease. Dis-ease is the subtle precursor to disease. It is not being comfortable in your physical body. Many people believe that 'psychosomatic' means that the illness is a fabrication of the mind. This is not so. Psychosomatic means that emotions and mental attitudes are affecting the physical body and causing disease, a situation which crystals can improve.

Red Jasper

The mind is closely involved in crystal healing. Belief in the process speeds things up, but you do not have to believe, merely to keep an open mind. The Tibetans, like many ancient peoples, have used crystals for thousands of years, and see closed-mindedness as one of the major causes of disease. They also believe, as do many Western doctors, that the body has a natural tendency towards wellness and that, if you listen to your body, you will instinctively know what is good for you. So, when you are attracted to a particular crystal, it will be because that crystal has properties that resonate with what your body or psyche needs.

HOW CRYSTALS WORK

Crystals work through the transmission of energy and the adjustment of subtle vibrations. Crystals absorb, focus, transmute and transmit electromagnetic energy; after all, they have lain within the Earth's magnetic field for millennia. They are like cosmic transceivers, stepping cosmic energy down from the spiritual level so that it can be absorbed and used by the physical body. It is not certain, though, how this energy is passed between the crystal and the human body.

The subtle bodies (collectively known as the aura, biomagnetic sheath or etheric body) that surround the physical body are formed from energies that have a lighter vibration than the physical body and are therefore invisible, but the physical body itself, which consists largely of water – an excellent medium for the transmission of vibration – carries extremely subtle vibrational signals through its nerves and neural pathways. Each of the different bodies in the aura (see page 16) has a subtle grid, similar to that used in acupuncture, known as the meridians, and crystals open up these pathways and dissolve blockages wherever they occur. The subtle bodies are linked to the physical body by the chakras, centres that mediate and distribute energy. But these can themselves become blocked, leading to subtle dis-ease, which if not brought back into equilibrium eventually leads to physical disease.

CAUSES OF DIS-EASE

- **Damaged immune system** Your immune system is the front line of defence against disease. If it is not functioning well, then dis-ease and organisms invade the body.

- **Shock or attack** If you receive a shock, whether it is at the physical, emotional or mental level, your chakras go out of balance and your body reacts. If you are attacked, whether by viruses or by someone's thoughts, dis-ease results.

- **Stress and tension** Anything that puts a continual stress on your system and causes inadequate rest will ultimately manifest as physical illness.

- **Negative attitudes or emotions** How you think or feel is how you ultimately become in your physical body. Emotions such as guilt or suppressed anger are insidious forerunners of disease, as are low self-esteem or shame.

- **Emotional exhaustion** If you have been continually drained by a person or a situation then you have lowered resistance to disease.

- **Anxiety or fear** Chronic anxiety and continual fear weaken the body. Anxiety is usually accompanied by loss of appetite and irregular sleeping patterns, and is often exacerbated by smoking or drinking. If depression is involved, medication may suppress underlying feelings causing dis-ease.

ABOVE **A crystal on the brow quickly eases a tension headache.**

ACTIVATING AND CARING FOR YOUR CRYSTALS

The 12 crystal healers in this book, which make up your crystal toolkit, have been specially chosen to cover as wide a spectrum of conditions as possible, but before they can begin to work for you, the crystals need to be activated and attuned to your particular frequency. The first step is a thorough cleanse to rid them of vibes they may have picked up before they reached you, and the second is an activation and blessing.

Orange Carnelian

Clear Quartz cluster

CLEANSING YOUR CRYSTALS

To cleanse your crystals, simply hold them under running water for a few minutes and then place them in the sun for a few hours. If there is no sun available, visualize bright white light radiating down onto the crystals.

It is most important that crystals are always cleansed after use for healing. However, if you keep your crystal healers together in a bag, the Clear Quartz and the Orange Carnelian will automatically cleanse the other crystals and transmute any negative energy that they may be holding.

ACTIVATING YOUR CRYSTALS

Hold all 12 crystals in your hands. Close your eyes and concentrate on the crystals. See them surrounded by bright white light. Ask that they will be attuned to your own unique frequency and that they will be activated to act as healers at any level you may need now or at any time in the future. Ask that the crystals be blessed by the highest energies in the universe and be dedicated to your self-healing and that of the environment around you.

CLOCKWISE FROM THE TOP **Amethyst, Soladite, Blue Lace Agate, Green Aventurine, Yellow Jasper, Orange Carnelian, Red Jasper, Bloodstone, Clear Quartz, Rose Quartz, Labrodorite and Smokey Quartz**

STORING YOUR CRYSTALS

The best way to store your healing stones is in a cloth bag. Tumbled stones are robust and do not easily scratch so the stones can be kept together ready for use at any time. You may wish to wear a particular crystal and you can do this in one of the purpose-made silver spirals obtainable from crystal stores. Alternatively, the crystal can be popped into a pocket, kept on your desk or by your bed. Be aware, however, that crystals that are worn or kept out in your environment will absorb negative energies and will therefore need regular cleansing.

GEM ELIXIRS

Gem elixirs are a simple and safe way to take in crystal energy. As crystals work by vibration and resonance, the energy can be easily transferred into spring water where it is stored until required. Gem elixirs can be taken internally or applied externally to affected areas; they can also be added to bathwater.

USING THE ELIXIR

- Sip the elixir at regular intervals or use to bathe the affected part. (Keep the elixir in a refrigerator when not in use.)

- If the elixir is to be kept more than a day, add one-third brandy or cider vinegar to the elixir as a preservative.

- To make a dosage bottle: add seven drops of the brandy elixir to a dropper bottle that has been filled with one-third brandy and two-thirds spring water. Take seven drops three times a day.

- A few drops of gem elixir can also be added to a spray bottle of water and spritzed around your home or workspace, or added to your bath.

MAKING A GEM ELIXIR

1. Cleanse your crystal before use (see page 10).

2. Place the crystal in a clean glass bowl. Cover the crystal with pure spring water.

3. Cover the bowl and place in the sun for 6 to 12 hours.

4. Remove the crystal. Pour the water into a clean glass bottle, and cap with an air-tight stopper.

ANATOMY

YOUR PHYSICAL ANATOMY

If you are not familiar with the anatomy of your physical body you will find it difficult to position your stones accurately over the appropriate organs. The illustrations below will help you to locate the organs and systems of the body.

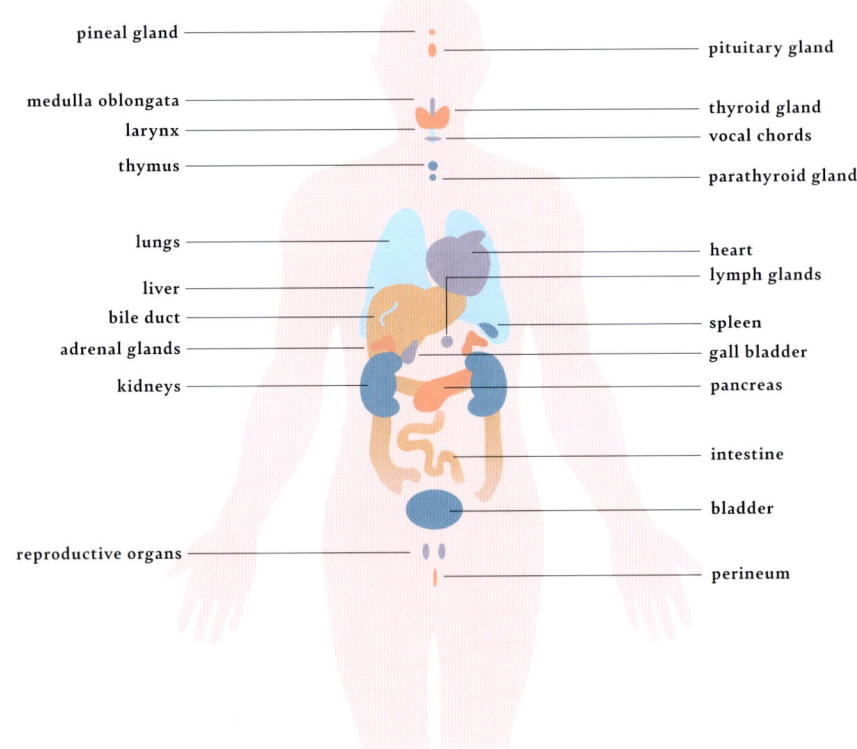

pineal gland — — pituitary gland

medulla oblongata — — thyroid gland
larynx — — vocal chords
thymus — — parathyroid gland

lungs — — heart
— lymph glands
liver —
bile duct — — spleen
adrenal glands — — gall bladder
kidneys — — pancreas

— intestine

— bladder

reproductive organs — — perineum

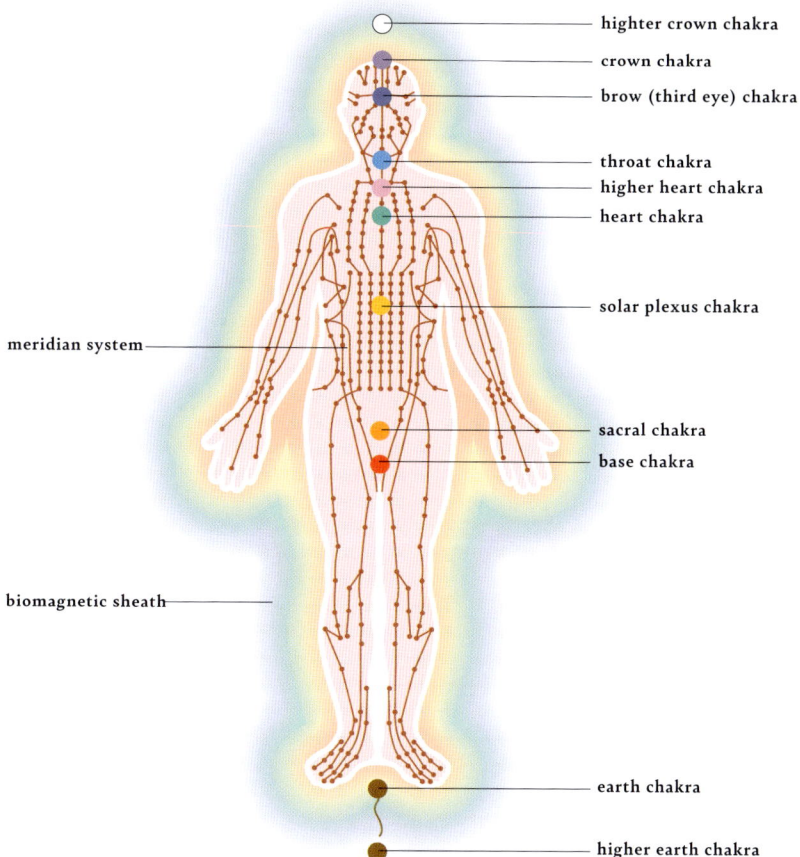

higher crown chakra

crown chakra

brow (third eye) chakra

throat chakra

higher heart chakra

heart chakra

solar plexus chakra

meridian system

sacral chakra

base chakra

biomagnetic sheath

earth chakra

higher earth chakra

YOUR SUBTLE ANATOMY

As well as your physical anatomy, your body has a subtle anatomy which is usually invisible to the naked eye. This consists of an etheric body made up of layers of biomagnetic energy, subtle DNA and a meridian system that conveys the life force around the bodies via chakra linkage points.

CRYSTALS AND YOUR CHAKRAS

The chakras are energy linkage centres that connect your physical body with the subtle bodies contained within the biomagnetic sheath, or aura, that surrounds your physical body. The chakras distribute the life force through the physical and subtle bodies. Each chakra is associated with a specific colour and crystal and governs different aspects of human emotion and behaviour. If a chakra becomes blocked, the subtle energy flow becomes imbalanced, and dis-ease or disharmony on the physical, emotional, mental or spiritual level eventually results.

Traditionally, there are seven major chakras, but more chakras are coming into play as the vibrations of the planet and the human body are stepped up to a higher frequency. This book uses crystals that activate five further chakras that will enhance your spiritual wellbeing and assist you to open your intuition and attune more strongly to the vibrational changes taking place.

An essential base for holistic healing, chakras create a state of harmony or disharmony, depending on how well each chakra is functioning, and on pages 20–21 you will find an exercise for cleansing, balancing and recharging all your chakras.

Specific issues and positive or negative qualities aligned to a particular chakra (see the chart on pages 18–19) can be supported or improved by placing the appropriate crystal on the chakra. If you have emotional, mental or spiritual issues connected to a specific chakra, your overall health will benefit from placing the crystal on the chakra and leaving it in place for 20 minutes or so while you relax quietly.

Yellow Jasper

THE 12 CHAKRAS AND ASSOCIATED CRYSTALS

	CHAKRA	CRYSTAL	FUNCTION
	Higher earth	Bloodstone	Cleansing and stabilizing
	Earth	Smoky Quartz	Grounding and protecting
	Base	Red Jasper	Energizing
	Sacral	Orange Carnelian	Creating
	Solar plexus	Yellow Jasper	Nurturing
	Heart	Green Aventurine	Healing emotional distress
	Higher heart	Rose Quartz	Unconditional love
	Throat	Blue Lace Agate	Opening communication
	Brow (third eye)	Sodalite	Attuning
	Crown	Amethyst	Opening intuition
	Higher crown (1)	Labradorite	Opening spiritual communication
	Higher crown (2)	Clear Quartz	Reaching enlightenment

THE CHAKRAS

CHAKRA	COLOUR	POSITION	BODY	ISSUE
Earth and Higher earth	Brown	Below feet	Physical	Material
Base	Red	Base of spine	Physical	Survival instincts
Sacral	Orange	Below navel	Physical	Creativity and procreation
Solar plexus	Yellow	Above navel	Emotional	Emotional connection and assimiliation
Heart	Green	Over heart	Emotional	Love
Higher heart	Pink	Over thymus	Links all	Unconditional live
Throat	Blue	Throat	Links emotional to mental	Communication
Brow (third eye)	Dark blue	Forehead	Mental	Intuition and mental connection
Crown	Violet	Top of head	Spiritual	Spiritual connection
Higher crown	White	Above head	Spiritual	Spiritual enlightenment

POSITIVE QUALITIES	NEGATIVE QUALITIES
Grounded, practical, operates well in everyday reality	Ungrounded, no sense of personal power, cannot operate in everyday reality, picks up negativity
Basical security, sense of one's own power, active, independent, spontaneous leadership	Impatience, fear of annihilation, death wish, over-sexed or impotent, vengeful, hyperactive, highly impulsive, anger, violence, manipulative
Fertility, courage, assertive, confident, joy, sexuality, sensual pleasure, acceptance of sexual identity	Low self-esteem, infertility, cruelty, sluggishness, inferiority, pompous, emotional hooks or thought forms
Good energy utilization, empathetic, organization, logic, active intelligence	Poor energy utilization, lazy, overly emotional or cold, cynical, emotional baggage, energy leaching, takes on other people's feelings and problems
Loving, generous, compassionate, nurturing, flexible, self-confident, accepting	Disconnected from feelings, unable to show love, jealous, possessive, insecure, miserly or resistant to change
Compassionate, empathetic, nurturing, forgiving, spiritually connected	Spiritually disconnected, grieving, inability to express feelings, needy
Able to speak own truth, receptive, idealistic, loyal	Unable to verbalize thoughts or feelings, stuck, dogmatic, disloyal
Intuitive, perceptive, visionary, in-the-moment	Spaced-out, fearful, attached to the past, superstitious, bombarded with other people's thoughts
Mystical, creative, humanitarian, giving service	Overly-imaginative, illusory, arrogant, uses power to control others
Spiritual, attuned to higher things, enlightened, true humilitiy	Spaced-out and open to invasion, illusions and delusions

CRYSTALS FOR CLEANSING AND RECHARGING YOUR CHAKRAS

People who are intuitive can see, or feel, chakras spinning, looking like whirling Catherine wheels of light. Dull or black patches, or a spin that 'wobbles' or is too fast or slow, indicates dis-ease at the physical, emotional, mental or spiritual level according to the chakra concerned. Fortunately, you do not need to 'see' such dis-ease because a crystal will pick up any disharmony, put it right and re-energize the chakra.

You can either do a complete chakra cleanse and recharge, as shown here, or you can cleanse one chakra if you particularly identify with the issue or qualities shown for that chakra on the chart on pages 18–19, or if you have an illness associated with that chakra. Throat or lung conditions, for instance, respond to treating the throat chakra, and abdominal distress to treating the base or sacral chakra.

FULL CHAKRA CLEANSE, BALANCE AND RECHARGE

1. Lie down comfortably. As you place each crystal in turn, picture light and energy radiating out from the crystal into the chakra for 2 or 3 minutes. Be aware that the chakra is being cleansed and its spin regulated.

- Place *Smoky Quartz* between and slightly below your feet on your earth chakra.

- Place *Red Jasper* on your base chakra.

- Place *Orange Carnelian* on your sacral chakra.

- Place *Yellow Jasper* on your solar plexus chakra.

- Place *Green Aventurine* on your heart chakra.

- Place *Blue Lace Agate* on your throat chakra.

- Place *Sodalite* on your brow chakra.

- Place *Amethyst* on your crown chakra.

2. Now take your attention slowly from the soles of your feet up the midline of your body, feeling how each chakra has become balanced and harmonized.

3. Remain still and relaxed, breathing deep down into your belly and counting to seven before you exhale. As you breathe in and hold, feel the energy of the crystals re-energizing the chakras and from there radiating out through your whole being.

4. When you feel ready, gather your crystals up, starting from the crown. As you reach the earth chakra, be aware of a grounding cord anchoring you to the earth and to your physical body.

5. Cleanse the crystals after use.

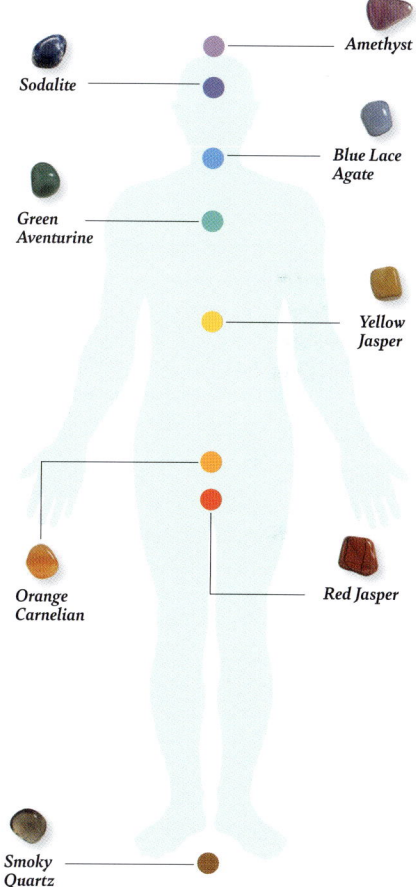

Amethyst

Sodalite

Blue Lace
Agate

Green
Aventurine

Yellow
Jasper

Orange
Carnelian

Red Jasper

Smoky
Quartz

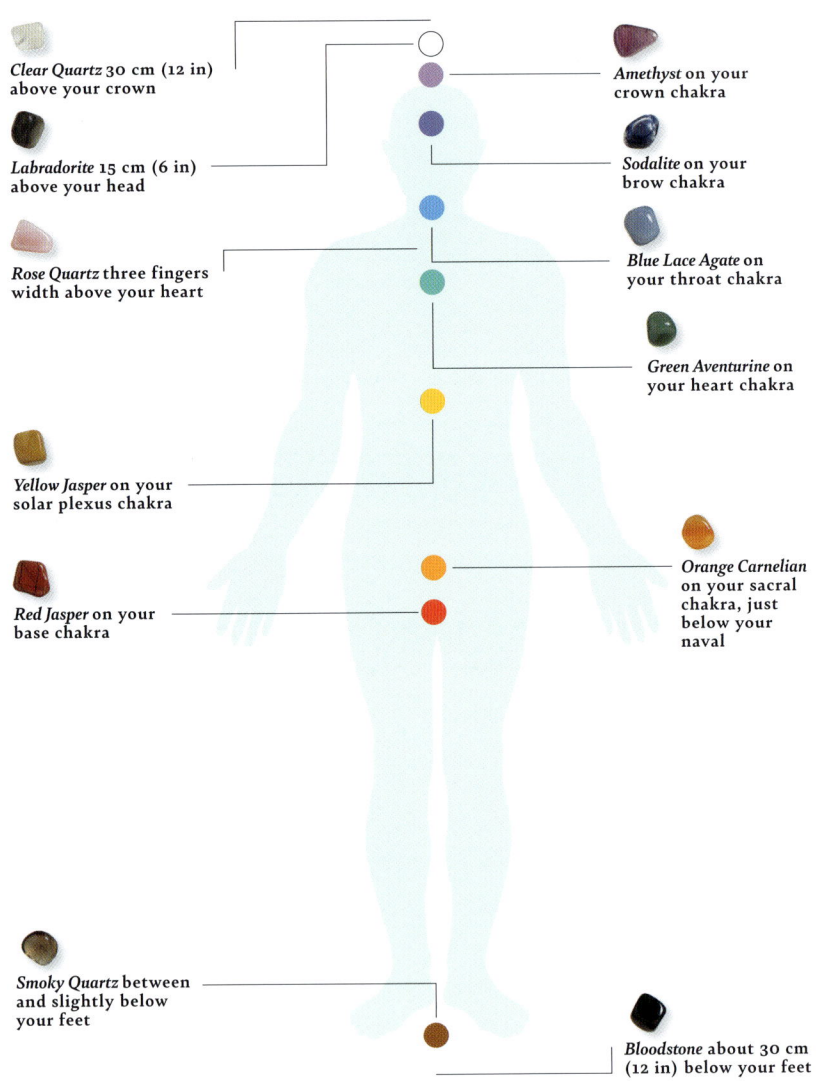

Clear Quartz 30 cm (12 in) above your crown

Labradorite 15 cm (6 in) above your head

Rose Quartz three fingers width above your heart

Yellow Jasper on your solar plexus chakra

Red Jasper on your base chakra

Smoky Quartz between and slightly below your feet

Amethyst on your crown chakra

Sodalite on your brow chakra

Blue Lace Agate on your throat chakra

Green Aventurine on your heart chakra

Orange Carnelian on your sacral chakra, just below your naval

Bloodstone about 30 cm (12 in) below your feet

ACTIVATING YOUR HIGHER CHAKRAS

1. Hold all 12 crystals in your hands for a few moments, visualizing them bathed in bright white light. Lie down comfortably and position the crystals as shown, starting at your feet. You may need some assistance.

2. Take your attention down to the *Bloodstone* and be aware of the higher earth chakra opening. Feel how it pulls in refined earth energies and radiates them up to the *Smoky Quartz* and through your whole body. Be aware of your connection to the Earth's biomagnetic sheath. Feel yourself aligning to the faster and purer vibration that it carries, and how it connects to the base chakras.

3. Now take your attention up to the *Rose Quartz*. Feel how the higher heart chakra opens and expands, receiving and radiating unconditional love and awakening your innate compassion and connection with others. Feel how this chakra connects to the throat chakra so that you can communicate love out to the world.

4. Finally, take your attention up to the *Clear Quartz* above your head. Be aware of its connection to higher spiritual guidance. Feel how the energy flows down into the *Labradorite*, activating its esoteric awareness and soul memory. Know that you are a spiritual being on a human journey.

5. When the activation is complete, slowly remove the crystals, starting with the highest crown chakra and working down to the earth chakra.

6. When you reach the earth chakra, be aware that there is a cord linking your feet to this chakra, grounding you within your physical body and connected to the earth.

7. Finally, pick up the *Bloodstone* from the higher earth chakra. Stand up and feel your feet firmly on the ground.

8. Repeat the exercise daily until the activation is complete.

STRENGTHENING YOUR AURA

Your aura, also known as the etheric body or biomagnetic sheath, is a subtle energy field that surrounds your physical body. Made up of several diffuse layers, the outer layer relates to spirit, the next layer to mind, the next to emotion and the one closest to the physical body relates to the physical level of being (see page 15).

Many people can catch a glimpse of this sheath as a white glow around someone, but to the intuitive eye the aura is a rainbow of colours swirling like a three-dimensional cloak anything from a hand's breadth to an arm's length out from the physical body. Within that rainbow, dark or dense patches indicate incipient or chronic disease.

Keeping your biomagnetic sheath as healthy as possible is an effective defence against illness and ensures your wellbeing on all levels. Clear Quartz is the crystal par excellence for strengthening your aura, and Smoky Quartz for cleansing it and drawing off negative energies.

You can train yourself to feel how far your aura extends and to check it for weak spots, but your crystals will do this for you automatically if you prefer.

Clear Quartz cluster

Smoky Quartz

Labradorite

AURA STRENGTHENING

1. Sit down quietly and place *Smoky Quartz* at your feet.

2. Place *Red Jasper* beneath you as close to your perineum as possible.

3. Hold *Labradorite* in your left hand.

4. Close your eyes, breathe gently, focussing your attention into your right hand. Extend your right arm to its full length with your palm facing into your body or hold your *Clear Quartz* in this hand. Move your hand slowly towards your body. At some point your hand will start to tingle and you will be aware of your subtle energy field (this may take a little practice). Note how far this field extends from your body. Move your hand around to see if you can detect any 'cold' or weak spots. If you do, leave the crystal over the spot for a few moments.

5. With *Clear Quartz* 'comb' your body from the top of your head working down the front midline of your body to your feet first, then down the outside of your body on each side, and finally down your back.

6. Repeat the 'combing' with the *Labradorite* in your left hand.

7. Position your *Clear Quartz* in front of your solar plexus for a few minutes to energize your aura.

8. Remember to cleanse the crystals after use.

CRYSTALS FOR YOUR BODY

Sodalite

Your immune system is your first line of defence against invading organisms. If it is working well and is balanced, you will have a quicker recovery time from minor illnesses such as colds and flu. However, some illnesses, such as myalgic encephalomyelitis (ME) and viral infections, are caused because the immune system is underactive and others, such as rheumatoid arthritis and lupus, because it is overactive. Crystals find the right balance. The major healing point for your immune system is over the thymus gland, located in the centre of your chest about a hand's breadth below your collarbone, but the spleen may also need support.

Bloodstone is an excellent stone for the immune system because of its amphoteric effect – this means that if the immune system is overactive, Bloodstone sedates it; if it is underactive, this crystal stimulates it. At the first sign of a cold, flu or other infectious or bacterial illness, tape a Bloodstone over your thymus and leave it in place for several hours.

To stimulate the immune system, place an immune stimulator on your thymus and a Clear Quartz in the centre of your forehead, and lie with your hands in your groin crease on both sides for 10 minutes.

IMMUNE STIMULATORS

Amethyst, Bloodstone, Clear Quartz, Green Aventurine, Rose Quartz, Sodalite

Bloodstone

DETOXIFICATION

If your body is toxic, it cannot maintain health. Stimulating your liver with the detoxification layout releases toxins and encourages your lymphatic system to remove them, bringing about a physical cleansing. A Yellow Jasper at your solar plexus stimulates an emotional detox as well.

DETOX LAYOUT

1. Lie down comfortably

- Place *Sodalite* at base of throat

- Place *Bloodstone* and *Amethyst* over thymus

- Place *Yellow Jasper* over solar plexus

- Place *Red Jasper* over liver

- Place *Smoky Quartz* between feet

2. Leave them in position for 15 to 20 minutes, or tape them on overnight.

3. Cleanse the crystals thoroughly.

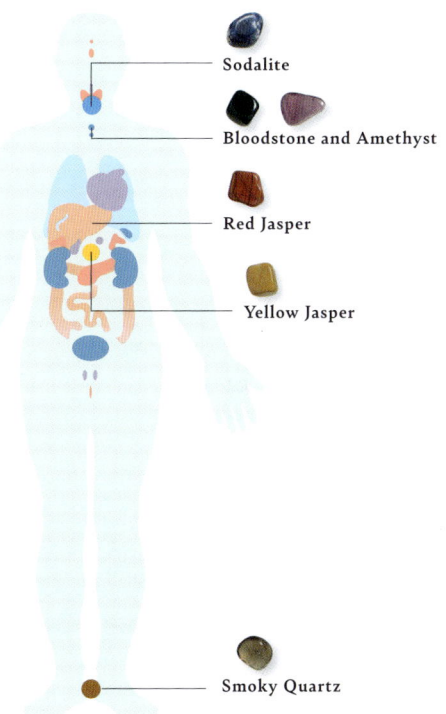

Sodalite

Bloodstone and Amethyst

Red Jasper

Yellow Jasper

Smoky Quartz

GROUNDING

One of the most widespread causes of feeling vaguely unwell and out of sorts is being ungrounded. Ungroundedness means you are not fully in your physical body, you are not in the present moment and your energy is scattered in all directions. Fortunately, a simple exercise as you leave your bed in the morning will get you focused and into your body.

THREE-MINUTE GROUNDING

1. Sit with your feet firmly on the floor. Hold a *Smoky Quartz* crystal in your left hand and place it over your sacral chakra just below your navel. Slowly breathe in for the count of five, hold it for the count of three, and breathe out for the count of seven. Repeat seven times. As you breathe, you will feel the energy from the *Smoky Quartz* centring itself in your sacral chakra, the centre of your body. Tell yourself firmly: 'I am centred and at one with my body.'

2. Place the *Smoky Quartz* between your feet. Stand up and be aware of your connection to the earth chakra which anchors you gently into your physical body. Tell yourself: 'I am focused and at one with the earth.'

3. Pick up your crystal and start your day.

Smoky Quartz

VITALITY

Red and orange are excellent colours for instilling vitality and *joie de vivre*, and for overcoming energy depletion. In your crystal toolkit you have two amazingly powerful stones: Orange Carnelian and Red Jasper. Both are strongly connected to the life force and to the lower chakras that assist the flow of the life force within your physical body. Carnelian is the stone for instant energy. Simply holding it for a few minutes charges you up; it is sensible to keep one in your pocket whenever you need a quick boost. Red Jasper provides you with a store of energy to draw on in the longer term and placed on your base chakra for 20 minutes, will give a boost to your sexual libido should this be flagging. Bloodstone, too, is a powerful revitalizer; hold it whenever you need a recharge.

Your crystal toolkit also contains the master energizer for the biomagnetic sheath: Clear Quartz. Energizing the biomagnetic sheath has an overall beneficial effect on your energy level in general, but also makes your physical body feel more vibrant. Hold it across your body, just below the navel, for 10 to 15 minutes.

Scintillating Labradorite provides a shot of spiritual vitality by connecting you to vibrant universal energies. These then pour down through your crown chakra into your spiritual body and from there into your physical self. Place it over the crown chakra for 10 to 15 minutes.

RIGHT **Hold a crystal whenever you need to recharge.**

CRYSTAL HEALING LAYOUT

There are several geometric shapes that can be laid out on or around the body to bring balance and healing.

One of the simplest is the five-pointed star. This grounds healing energy down into the body and balances and energizes it. The stones used can be chosen according to the condition, organs or systems involved (see pages 118–125), in which case you would place appropriate stones in positions 6 and 7 on the illustration, or use the same crystal for all points, or you can do a general healing layout as shown opposite. If you do not have anyone to lay out the stones for you, tape 3, 4, 6 and 7 in place.

NON-SPECIFIC HEALING LAYOUT

1. *Clear Quartz* above head to restore the body to its most perfect energetic state.

2. *Smoky Quartz* at right foot to ground.

3. *Orange Carnelian* on left palm to recharge the body.

4. *Yellow Jasper* on right palm to nurture and detoxify.

5. *Labradorite* at left foot to ground spiritual energies.

6. *Bloodstone* under right collarbone to stimulate the immune system.

7. *Blue Lace Agate* under left collarbone to stabilize and balance the body.

8. *Red Jasper* below perineum to provide a reservoir of energy.

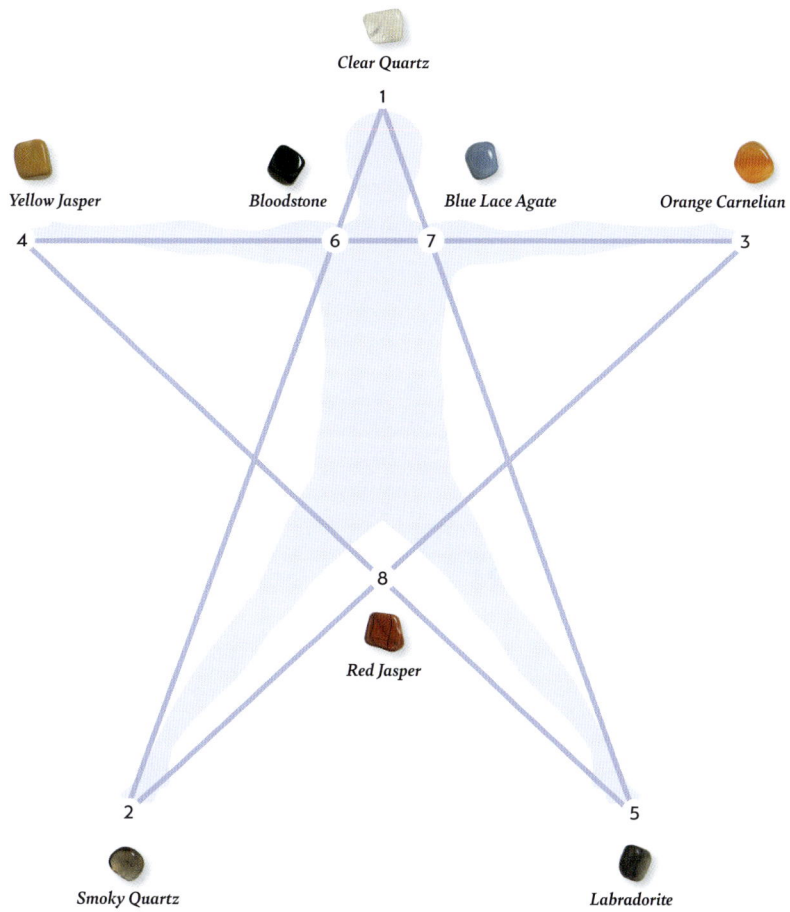

Clear Quartz

1

Yellow Jasper   Bloodstone   Blue Lace Agate   Orange Carnelian

4   6   7   3

8

Red Jasper

2   5

Smoky Quartz   Labradorite

CRYSTALS FOR YOUR MIND

Crystals have a powerful effect on your mind, calming an overactive mind and stimulating a sluggish one. They promote concentration, focus and creativity.

CRYSTALS TO IMPROVE CONCENTRATION, FOCUS, MEMORY AND LEARNING

Cool and calming Amethyst focuses the mind and improves your memory, while vibrant Carnelian sharpens your concentration and dispels mental lethargy. The rarified vibrations of Labradorite combine intellectual thought with intuition, and gazing into its iridescent depths calms an overactive mind. Clear Quartz focuses your concentration and unlocks memory. Hold it to your forehead for a few moments to aid recall.

If positive, practical thought and insight are what you need, Smoky Quartz promotes these and helps you to resolve contradictions. This pragmatic stone brings your common sense to the fore and reduces communication difficulties.

Sodalite has a strong effect on the mind. It eliminates mental confusion and encourages rational thought and intuitive perception, opening your mind to receive new information.

If your mind has been overworked, Bloodstone's revitalizing properties are an excellent tonic. This stone reduces mental confusion and imparts mental alertness. Strengthening your ability to make decisions, Bloodstone helps you to adjust your mindset to adapt to changing or altered circumstances, maintaining your mental stability. Keeping a Bloodstone in your pocket during examinations or other stressful situations keeps your mind calm and able to focus on finding solutions rather than focussing on the problem.

The layout below is one example of how to use mind crystals. There are many other ways. Simply holding in the hand or wearing the crystals will work on the mind, or the crystal can be placed to the head or worn as earrings.

CONCENTRATION AND MEMORY IMPROVER LAYOUT

1. Place *Sodalite* high on your forehead.

2. Place *Clear Quartz* lower on the forehead.

3. Place *Labradorite* to your right.

4. Place *Smoky Quartz* to your left.

5. Leave the crystals in place for 15 to 20 minutes.

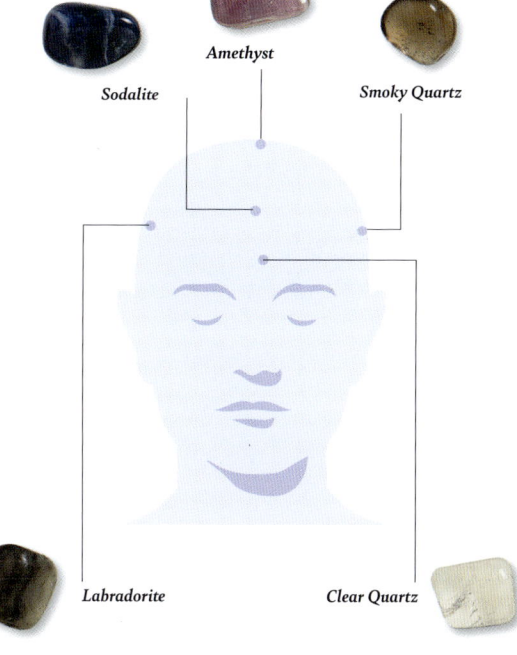

Amethyst

Sodalite

Smoky Quartz

Labradorite

Clear Quartz

PROBLEM-SOLVING AND CREATIVITY

Your creativity and capacity to solve problems can be expanded by uniting the two different hemispheres of your brain. The left side of the brain is the analytic, rational side, concerned with sequential, logical thought processes and the right side is the illogical, intuitive part that makes random leaps to find creative answers. Crystals connect the two hemispheres and harness their powers.

MANDALA MEDITATION

Placing crystals into a mandala, a regular pattern used for meditation, induces a state of mind in which creative solutions can easily rise to the surface. Sit quietly for a few minutes holding your crystals, clearly defining the problem. Then lay out the mandala in the numbered order shown.

1. Clear Quartz
2. Red Jasper
3. Bloodstone
4. Labradorite
5. Amethyst
6. Smoky Quartz
7. Rose Quartz
8. Yellow Carnelian
9. Blue Lace Agate
10. Sodalite
11. Carnelian
12. Green Aventurine

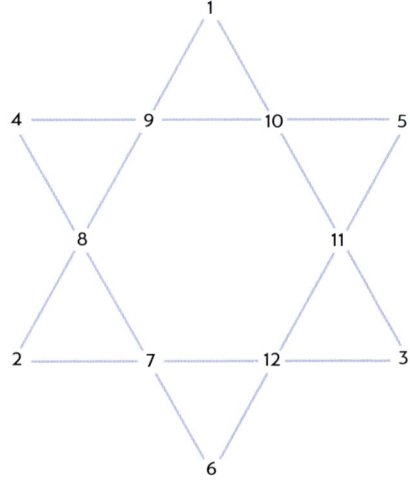

CRYSTALS FOR CREATIVITY

- **Amethyst** and **Bloodstone** facilitate the decision-making process, helping you to think laterally.

- **Blue Lace Agate** counteracts mental stress and encourages your mind to expand.

- **Carnelian** encourages your analytic abilities and sharpens your perception. It attunes day dreamers to everyday reality, uniting logic and intuition.

- **Clear Quartz** amplifies your thought power and brings about positive solutions.

- **Green Aventurine** stimulates your creativity and helps you to see alternative possibilities.

- **Labradorite** balances the rational mind with intuitive wisdom.

- **Red Jasper** or **Yellow Jasper** helps you get to grips with problems assertively. It combines organizational abilities with the imagination. Red Jasper brings hidden problems to light before they get too big, helping you to find new coping strategies, and provides insights into the most difficult of situations. Both Red and Yellow Jasper heighten creativity.

- **Rose Quartz** improves your ability to think and brings about mental clarity, encouraging your creativity.

- **Smoky Quartz** encourages positive thought and clear insights.

- **Sodalite** is an essential companion to creative thought. It clarifies your perceptions and releases you from bondage to a specific set of ideas, allowing you to assimilate new information and put the insights into practice.

Blue Lace Agate

HEALING MENTAL PROBLEMS

Crystals can be an enormous support if you suffer from mental problems or have minor psychiatric conditions. They can stabilize your mood, or assist you to overcome addictions, particularly as they help you deal with the underlying cause of your problem. Wear your stone constantly to support your mind and your intention to heal, and take the gem elixir (see page 13) three times a day.

CRYSTALS FOR HEALING MENTAL PROBLEMS

PROBLEM	CRYSTAL
Addictions	*Amethyst* has a sobering effect and is helpful in overcoming addictions or overindulgence of any kind (use non-alcoholic cider vinegar to preserve the gem elixir).
Alzheimer's	*Rose Quartz* is a useful stone for reducing the confusion of Alzheimer's and senile dementia.
Mid-life crisis	*Rose Quartz* will steer you through a mid-life crisis, enabling you to get your life back on track.
Panic attacks	*Sodalite* calms panic attacks. Keep it in your pocket and hold it over your chest at the first sign. Breathe slowly and deeply counting to seven, holding the breath in for a count of six, and then breathing out for a count of five.
Phobias	*Sodalite* is an excellent stone to help you overcome your phobias; *Green Aventurine* specifically overcomes claustrophobia.

PROBLEM	CRYSTAL
Psychiatric conditions	An effective balancer of mood and a natural tranquillizer, *Amethyst* can help to stabilize psychiatric conditions but should not be used for the treatment of paranoia or schizophrenia. This powerful healing stone is extremely calming for your mind, assisting you to feel less scattered.
Neurosis	*Green Aventurine* is beneficial in severe neurosis, helping you to understand what lies behind the condition.
Overly sensitive or defensive personality	*Sodalite* releases the core fears and control mechanisms that underlie this problem and enhances your self-acceptance.
Rigid mental conditioning	*Sodalite* gently releases your old mental conditioning and dissolves a rigid mindset allowing you to be more yourself.
Suicidal tendencies	The gently cleansing and protective energies of *Smoky Quartz* are excellent for alleviating suicidal urges as it resolves ambivalence about being in your physical body.

CRYSTALS FOR YOUR EMOTIONS

Wearing or surrounding yourself with crystals helps you keep your emotions in balance. The crystals gently release the emotional blockages or suppressed feelings that cause your moods to fluctuate.

EMOTIONAL 'RESCUE REMEDY'

Place a Rose Quartz over your heart, a Smoky Quartz over your solar plexus and an Amethyst over the higher heart chakra and leave in place for 20 minutes to restore emotional equilibrium.

CRYSTALS FOR EMOTIONAL BALANCE

- Amethyst balances out emotional highs and lows, encouraging emotional centring. It gently dissolves emotional blocks.

- Rose Quartz is the master healer for the emotions. Calming and reassuring, it strengthens empathy and sensitivity, helping you to understand how other people feel and how that affects you. This beautiful crystal releases unexpressed emotions and heals heartache, transmuting emotional conditioning that no longer serves you. It comforts grief and helps self-forgiveness and self-worth.

- Smoky Quartz stabilizes your emotions during emotional trauma or stress and dissolves negative emotions, allowing for emotional detoxification. This stone assists in tolerating difficult times with equanimity. It relieves fear and induces emotional calmness, and is useful if depression is pulling you down.

Amethyst

NEGATIVE EMOTIONS AND THE CHAKRAS

Placing the appropriately coloured stone on the corresponding chakra (see the table on pages 18–19) helps to change negative emotions into positive ones. As the negative emotion will be deeply ingrained, the crystal can be taped in place, or this exercise repeated at least once daily for a week or more.

NEGATIVE EMOTION	CHAKRA	CRYSTAL	POSITIVE EMOTION
Powerlessness	Earth	Smoky Quartz	Empowerment
Insecurity	Base	Red Jasper	Security
Low self-esteem	Sacral	Orange Carnelian	Self-confidence
Inferiority	Solar plexus	Yellow Jasper	Empathy
Jealousy	Heart	Green Aventurine	Compassion
Neediness	Higher heart	Rose Quartz	Unconditional love
Disloyalty	Throat	Blue Lace Agate	Loyalty
Self-delusion	Brown	Sodalite	Emotional clarity
Arrogance	Crown	Clear Quartz	Joy

HEALING DEPRESSION

Depression is an extremely debilitating emotional state that manifests somewhat differently according to its cause. Wear a crystal according to the type of depression you are experiencing or sip the gem elixir (see page 13) at regular intervals throughout the day.

Reactive depression occurs in response, or as a reaction, to life events. It is triggered by a stressful condition in the family or a personal situation, but it may also be linked to emotional blockages or suppressed memories. It is common in partners of people who suffer from depression. Reactive depression is alleviated by happy events or by removal of the stressful situation. Typically, symptoms are less noticeable in the morning and increase during the day. Endogenous depression is not alleviated by happy events and is believed to be caused by biochemical imbalances, although emotional factors or spiritual dis-ease will also be present. The sufferer has disturbed sleep and eating patterns and wakes feeling very low.

CRYSTALS FOR DEPRESSION

- Labradorite benefits reactive depression, where life events and stressful situations create the depression, and steers you through necessary change.

- Smoky Quartz is useful for endogenous depression and alleviates suicidal tendencies. This stone gently dissolves any negative emotions or emotional blockages that underlie depression.

Labradorite

LAYOUT FOR ALLEVIATING DEPRESSION

1. Lie comfortably on your bed or on the floor. Ensure that you will not be disturbed.

2. Place an *Amethyst* on your brow to balance out emotional highs and lows and to promote emotional centering.

3. Place *Rose Quartz* over your heart to release unexpressed emotions and heartache, soothe your emotional pain and open your heart to unconditional love.

4. Place *Smoky Quartz* or *Labradorite* on your solar plexus to draw out fear and negative emotions, encouraging you to let go of anything that no longer serves you, and instilling positive vibes in its place.

5. Place *Orange Carnelian* on your sacral chakra to stabilize and anchor you into the present. Feel the vibrant energy of the stone radiating up through your whole body and down into the sexual chakras to heal abuse of any kind.

6. Leave the stones in place for 15 to 20 minutes and then sit up slowly.

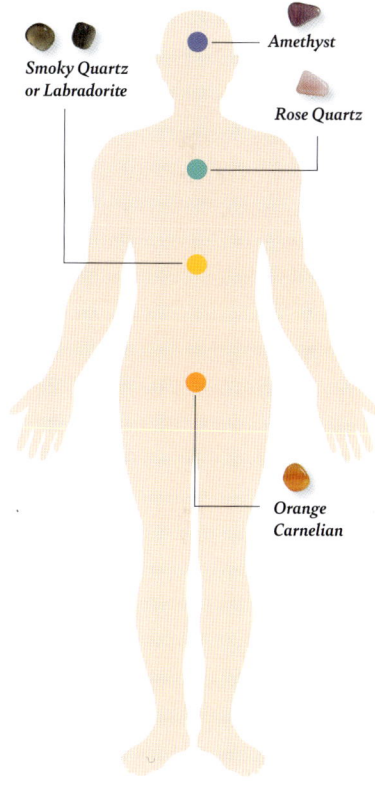

Smoky Quartz or Labradorite

Amethyst

Rose Quartz

Orange Carnelian

HEALING NEGATIVE EMOTIONS

Crystals draw out difficult emotions. They can be taken as a gem elixir (see page 13) or placed over the appropriate chakra. As the crystal is placed, visualize it pulling the negative emotion from your physical body and the subtle bodies, and then filling the space with the crystal's unique healing vibration.

CRYSTALS FOR ANGER (BASE CHAKRA)

- **Blue Lace Agate** gently dissolves anger, replacing it with profound peace.

- **Carnelian** calms anger and is helpful for moving beyond abuse (which can also cause feelings of impotence and powerlessness).

- **Amethyst** dispels anger and deep-seated rage, transmuting it into a loving energy, and can dispel the grief that often underlies rage.

- **Bloodstone** reduces irritability, aggressiveness and impatience, and all forms of anger.

- **Green Aventurine** calms anger and irritation and promotes an overall feeling of wellbeing in its place.

CRYSTALS FOR HEALING PAST HURTS (BASE, SACRAL, SOLAR PLEXUS, HEART AND THROAT CHAKRAS)

- **Blue Lace Agate** releases you from situations where you felt rejected and, helps you to accept the sensitivity for which you may have been ridiculed in the past.

- **Amethyst** dispels fear and anxiety and alleviates sadness and grief. It helps adjust to any loss you may have suffered, wiping away pain and grief.

CRYSTALS FOR GUILT (BASE, SOLAR PLEXUS AND BROW CHAKRAS)

- **Blue Lace Agate** releases your suppressed feelings and frees you from the judgement so often a part of parent-child relationships, and which is a source of guilt.

CRYSTALS FOR FORGIVENESS (HIGHER HEART CHAKRA)

- The gentle energies of **Rose Quartz** help you to forgive both yourself and other people. This stone of unconditional love and acceptance brings about deep forgiveness and instils spiritual peace.

- **Green Aventurine** is a stone of compassion and empathy that helps you to forgive other people.

FORGIVENESS RITUAL

1. Hold your *Rose Quartz* over your higher heart chakra.

2. Picture the person who you feel you need to forgive or from whom you seek forgiveness (you can use a photograph if you have one).

3. Be aware of the unconditionally loving energy of the *Rose Quartz* radiating out into your higher heart chakra and from there into your heart. Be aware that this energy is also pouring into the other person's heart.

4. Say out loud: 'I forgive you and I accept your forgiveness. I offer you unconditional love and acceptance. Go in peace.'

5. When you feel ready, put down the crystal.

Rose Quartz

REVITALIZE YOUR SEX LIFE

Sexual activity is linked to the lower chakras, and when these are cleansed and energized, libido is able to flow freely. Crystals activate these centres and also those of the emotional body so that love can be given and exchanged freely. Your sex life can be greatly enhanced if you and your partner share the sexual recharge ritual, placing the stones on each other as part of your foreplay or enfolding them between your bodies if this is comfortable for you.

CRYSTALS FOR LOVE

- **Red Jasper** is an excellent stone for stimulating your libido and for prolonging your sexual pleasure. Red Jasper energizes and cleanses the base chakra.

- **Orange Carnelian** is a recharging crystal. It energizes the sacral chakra, overcomes impotence or frigidity, and restores vitality to the female reproductive organs.

- **Smoky Quartz** helps you to accept that you are in a physical body with normal and natural sexual impulses. It enhances virility and cleanses the base chakras so that your passion can flow freely.

- **Rose Quartz** opens your heart chakra and restores love and trust between you and your partner. It teaches you how to love yourself and to receive love from someone else. This stone is said to increase your fertility.

Red Jasper

THE SEXUAL RECHARGE

1. Lie down comfortably.

2. Place a *Rose Quartz* over your heart to open it to receive love.

3. Place *Smoky Quartz* between your thighs so that your passion can flow freely.

4. Place *Red Jasper* at the base of your pubic bone to stimulate your libido and cleanse the base chakra. This stone prolongs sexual pleasure.

5. Place *Orange Carnelian* on your sacral chakra to cleanse it and open your creative energy.

6. Leave the stones in place for 10 to 15 minutes.

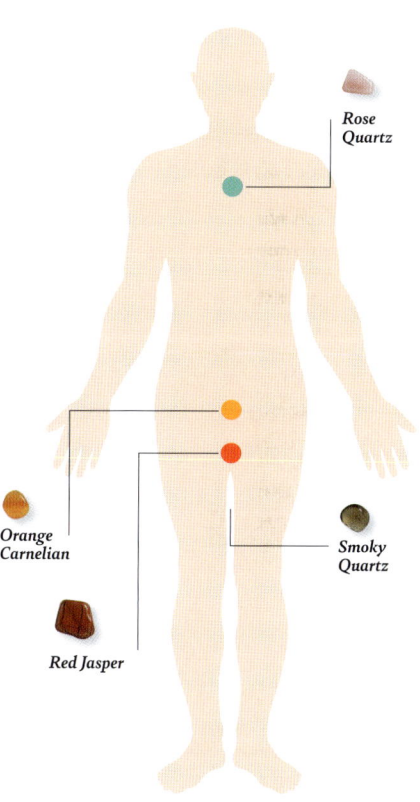

Rose
Quartz

Orange
Carnelian

Smoky
Quartz

Red Jasper

CRYSTALS FOR YOUR SPIRIT

As they are full of spiritual energy and light, crystals work brilliantly to heal or support your spirit and to open your intuition. The high-vibration crystals such as the Quartzes and Labradorite work through the spiritual body to ground spiritual energy into the physical body and to bring about profound insights.

CRYSTALS FOR INTUITION AND INSIGHT

Hold one of the five intuition crystals to your third eye whenever you need spiritual sight or intuitive guidance or a glimpse into the future.

- **Labradorite** works in two ways to enhance intuition. Firstly, Labradorite brings messages from the unconscious mind to the surface and helps you to intuitively understand these. Secondly, it accesses other lives and other worlds, bringing intuitive wisdom into your awareness. Labradorite is particularly useful when you want to get to the bottom of things and to understand the real motivation behind other people's thoughts and actions.

- **Sodalite** unites logic with intuition. It opens spiritual perception and brings information from the higher mind down to the everyday mind. This stone stimulates the pineal gland and deepens your awareness.

RIGHT **Hold a crystal to your third eye to stimulate your intuition.**

- **Clear Quartz** acts rather like a computer. It stores information and is a spiritual library waiting to be accessed. This stone enhances intuition and psychic abilities. It has been used since time immemorial as a scrying stone to take you into the future or the past.

- **Amethyst** is one of the great heighteners of intuition and spiritual awareness. The serene energies of Amethyst take you to a different plane. It is an excellent stone for gazing into as a scrying tool and can be placed on the third eye to open it.

- **Smoky Quartz** brings spiritual energies down to earth. Smoky Quartz can be used as a scrying stone to focus intuition. Simply hold your crystal and gaze into its depths, allowing your eyes to go out of focus. Notice what drifts into your mind.

INTUITION LAYOUT

1. Lie down comfortably.

2. Place *Clear Quartz* about a hand's breadth above your head.

3. Place *Amethyst* just touching your crown.

4. Place *Labradorite* on the top of your forehead.

5. Place *Sodalite* between your eyebrows.

6. Leave the crystals in place for 15 minutes.

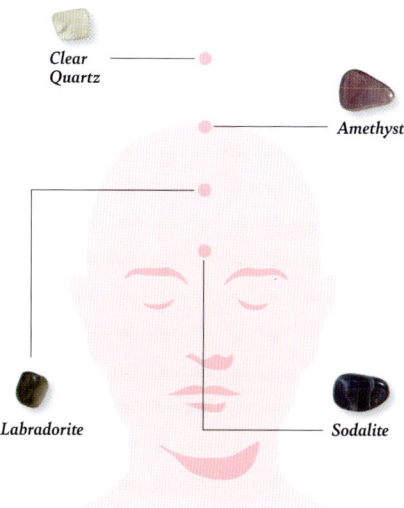

Clear Quartz

Amethyst

Labradorite

Sodalite

HEALING DREAMS

Crystals can be programmed to bring you healing dreams. Simply hold your crystal in your hands for a few moments, visualizing it surrounded by light. Firmly state your intention that your crystal will bring you a healing dream that you will remember and understand on waking. Then place the crystal under your pillow before you go to sleep. Keep a pad and pen by the bed to write down your dream.

CRYSTALS FOR DREAMING

- **Red Jasper** and **Yellow Jasper** assist you in recalling significant dreams. Jasper helps the subconscious mind to communicate with the conscious mind in the dream state.

- **Bloodstone** stimulates dreaming.

- **Amethyst** makes intuitive dreams and journeys out of the body easier and helps you in understanding your dreams. An Amethyst under your pillow guards against nightmares and ensures sweet dreams.

RIGHT **Slip a crystal under your pillow to stimulate insightful dreams or sound sleep.**

MEETING THE DREAM HEALER

1. A simple visualization before going to bed will put you in touch with the dream healer. Sit or lie down, whichever is more comfortable.

2. Holding an *Amethyst* in your hands to enhance your visualization abilities, sit quietly and close your eyes. Breathe gently and evenly, establishing a natural rhythm and withdrawing your attention into yourself.

3. Without opening your eyes, raise them so that you are looking at your third eye in the centre of your forehead. Picture this eye opening and revealing a beautiful place into which you can step. (If you find this difficult initially, place your *Amethyst* on your third eye to stimulate its opening.)

4. Spend a few moments exploring and enjoying this beautiful place. As you explore, you will become aware that there is a figure joining you. This figure is the dream healer (it is not necessarily human).

5. Explain to the dream healer exactly what kind of healing you need, whether it is physical, emotional, mental or spiritual. If you don't know the source of your dis-ease, then ask the dream healer to tune in and give you the right kind of healing. Request that tonight you will receive healing and that on waking you will recall your dream clearly and will know exactly what it means.

6. When you go to bed, place your *Amethyst* under your pillow. Tell yourself firmly that you will be meeting the dream healer and that you will remember your dream.

7. When you wake up, write the dream down and any insights you have about it.

CRYSTAL MEDITATION

Meditation switches off the mind and puts you in touch with spiritual reality. Gazing into the depths of a clear crystal enables you to quickly enter a meditative state. Crystals have a natural affinity with meditation as they calm your mind and open it to receive spiritual energy. Your brain puts out different electrical frequencies, known as brain waves, according to your state of consciousness. Holding a Smoky Quartz crystal can help you to move between the beta brain waves of everyday awareness and the alpha brain waves produced during meditation and altered states.

CRYSTALS FOR MEDITATION

- **Smoky Quartz** enhances moving between alpha and beta brain wave states and calms your mind.

- **Sodalite** opens your higher awareness and stimulates spiritual perception, taking your meditation to a deeper level.

- *Clear Quartz* tunes out distractions and is an excellent aid to meditation. This stone naturally attunes itself to your vibration and then takes your energy back to a state of spiritual perfection.

MEDITATION

1. Settle yourself on a cushion in a quiet place, making sure that you will not be disturbed. Breathe gently and evenly, establishing a natural rhythm. As you breathe in, take in a sense of peace and let your body relax and soften. As you breathe out, let go of any tension or extraneous thoughts or anxieties. Allow your body and your mind to settle into a quiet space.

2. Using your crystal toolkit but keeping your *Labradorite* in reserve, make a crystal circle around yourself, working from the brown of *Smoky Quartz* through red, orange

and yellow to green and blue, then into *Amethyst* and *Clear Quartz*. Focus on each crystal in turn for a few moments before touching it to your third eye and then placing it in the circle.

3. Hold your *Labradorite* in your hands, turn it until it catches the light and gaze into its mysterious depths. Breathe more deeply into your belly, consciously grounding spiritual energy. Close your eyes. Let any thoughts or sounds drift past you and be aware only of the crystal in your hands, its energy and the insight that it brings to you.

4. After 10 to 20 minutes, gather up your crystals and place them to one side. Holding your *Smoky Quartz*, stand up and feel your feet firmly on the floor. Be aware of the grounding cord that goes from your feet deep down into the earth to hold you gently in your physical body.

Clear Quartz

Smoky Quartz

Red Jasper

Rose Quartz

Orange Carnelian

Amethyst

Yellow Jasper

Blue Lace Agate

Sodalite

Green Aventurine

CONNECTING WITH THE DIVINE

Connection with the divine energies and the spiritual level of being often occurs during meditation, when it is known as bliss consciousness or enlightenment, but you can be connected to divine energy all the time with the assistance of your crystal toolkit. Connecting to this energy and anchoring it into your crystal means that you will always be connected to the divine light at the heart of the universe.

CRYSTALS FOR THE SPIRIT

- **Labradorite**, a highly mystical stone, raises your consciousness to the highest possible level so that you can make contact with the divine. It then grounds the energies into your body. It carries esoteric knowledge to feed your soul.

- **Rose Quartz** is the stone of unconditional love. It takes you into the heart of the divine light. It helps you to recognize that you are a spiritual being whose true nature is divine, enhancing your spiritual awareness.

- **Blue Lace Agate** is a spiritually uplifting stone. It takes you on a journey through the cosmos to your divine home.

- **Clear Quartz** carries the vibration of divine light. Simply by holding Clear Quartz above your head for a few moments, you can experience an influx of spiritual energy that connects you directly with the divine.

TRAVELLING THE WAVES OF SPIRIT

Holding your Blue Lace Agate, be aware of the gentle curves that flow over its surface. These are the waves in the sea of spirit to which we all belong. Trace these curves with your eyes, letting them go a little out of focus. Travel the waves until you reach your spiritual home. Bring the stone to your throat and anchor the connection there.

ANCHORING DIVINE LIGHT

Holding your Labradorite and gazing into its depths be aware that the blue flashes that you glimpse are the light of the divine which are anchored into your crystal. Know that whenever you hold this crystal, you will have an immediate connection to the divine. Place the crystal to your forehead and absorb the divine light into your whole being.

ATTUNING TO UNCONDITIONAL LOVE

Holding your Rose Quartz, allow yourself to feel the unconditional love radiating out from its serene core. This is the love that is at the heart of the universe and which spreads through all things. Place the stone over your heart and allow your heart to absorb this unconditional, divine love, feeling it flood through your whole being.

RIGHT **Blue Lace Agate connects to the divine and takes you to your spiritual home.**

CRYSTALS FOR RELAXATION

Regular relaxation conveys an enormous benefit to your health and plays a major part in preventing disease. Crystals quieten your body, mind and emotions, bringing about a deep sense of calm and centredness. If you feel uptight, crystals will help you to unwind; if you feel physically jittery and cannot stay still, crystals will relax your muscles; and if your thoughts are racing, they will shut down your mind. Taking 15 or 20 minutes out of your day to relax with your crystals will bring you inner peace that radiates out into your daily life.

CRYSTALS FOR CALMING

- **Amethyst** is a natural tranquillizer. It induces a profound sense of peace and relaxation.

- **Blue Lace Agate** links your thought processes to the spiritual vibration. The serene energies of Blue Lace Agate induce profound peace of mind.

- **Clear Quartz** takes your vibrations back to a state of perfect balance. It acts as a deep soul cleanser and draws spiritual energies into the physical body.

- **Green Aventurine** is a comforter and heart healer. Green Aventurine imparts a sense of wellbeing and emotional serenity.

- **Rose Quartz**, a stone of infinite peace, draws off negative vibes, filling you with gentle healing energy.

- **Smoky Quartz** is an excellent stone for drawing off negativity and environmental stress. It also instils a deep sense of relaxation into the physical body.

- **Yellow Jasper** cleanses and aligns the subtle bodies. It brings about balance and instils the certainty of being nurtured and supported.

CRYSTAL RELAXATION LAYOUT

1. Lie down and make yourself comfortable. Ensure that you will not be disturbed. Turn off your phone.

2. Place *Clear Quartz* just above your head.

3. Place *Amethyst* on your forehead. (Tape in place if necessary).

4. Place *Blue Lace Agate* at your throat. (Tape if necessary).

5. Place *Rose Quartz* over your heart. (Tape if necessary).

6. Place *Yellow Jasper* over your solar plexus.

7. Place *Smoky Quartz* at your feet.

8. Close your eyes, breathe gently and leave the crystals in place for 15 or 20 minutes, then remove, starting with the top of the head. When you get to your feet, be aware of a grounding cord going from your feet deep into the earth to hold you in your physical body.

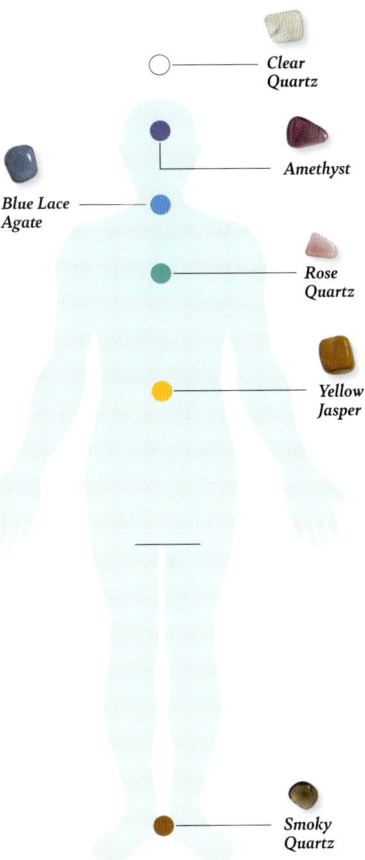

Clear Quartz

Amethyst

Blue Lace Agate

Rose Quartz

Yellow Jasper

Smoky Quartz

STRESS RELIEF

Stress, whether physical, emotional or mental, takes an enormous toll on your body, causing headaches, aches and pains, hot sweats, fatigue, insomnia, stomach ulcers and various auto-immune diseases. When you are under stress your adrenal glands, which sit on top of your kidneys, go into 'fight or flight' mode, over-producing adrenaline. This is nature's way of giving you additional strength to overcome occasional difficulties, but nowadays many people suffer continual stress, which results in burnout — if this adrenaline is not removed from your body, you end up feeling wired and find it impossible to sleep or relax. Lying quietly for 20 minutes with the appropriate crystal helps you to release stress, but you can also carry the crystal in your pocket and use it as a hand soother to play with whenever you need it.

CRYSTALS FOR RELIEVING STRESS

- **Green Aventurine** and **Rose Quartz** prevent the over-production of adrenaline and reduce the feeling of being wired. Green Aventurine aids mental stress and Rose Quartz emotional stress, but the two complement each other and work in tandem. Place (or tape) Rose Quartz on your left kidney and Green Aventurine on your right, slightly above your waist and either side of your spine. Leave in place for 20 minutes to reduce an adrenaline high.

- **Amethyst** is an excellent stone to use if stress is causing a tension headache. Place the Amethyst in the centre of your forehead, or at the back of your skull, and lie still, breathing in slowly for a count of six, holding it for six, and breathing out for a count of seven for 15 to 20 minutes.

- **Bloodstone** will keep your mind calm and focused during periods of mental stress, supporting your immune system at the same time.

- **Clear Quartz** and **Labradorite** are both useful stones to accompany you through emotional stress. Labradorite will gently bring up suppressed emotions that are contributing to your dis-ease, and Clear Quartz will energize you if stress is making you lethargic.

- **Rose Quartz** is an exceptionally calming stone that supports you during emotional trauma or crisis, giving you reassurance and helping you to accept necessary change.

- **Smoky Quartz** is a superb antidote to stress, particularly if it is caused by adverse environmental energies. Fortifying your resolve, it helps you to face difficult periods calmly, and protects against environmental stress.

- **Yellow Jasper** is an excellent stone if you feel you need support and nurturing during stressful periods. It instills tranquillity and has the added benefit of giving you the tenacity to overcome your difficulties.

RIGHT **Amethyst quickly dissipates the pain of a tension headache.**

INSOMNIA

Insomnia can arise from various causes, and there are several crystals that will assist you to sleep more deeply. The crystal can either be placed under your pillow, worn around your neck, or taken three times a day as a gem elixir (see pages 13) with an additional dose taken at bedtime and if you wake during the night.

CRYSTALS TO HELP YOU SLEEP

- **Amethyst** is the stone to use if your insomnia is caused by an overactive mind or by recurrent nightmares. A natural tranquillizer, Amethyst calms your mind and allows you to put aside thoughts of the day. If you suffer from recurrent nightmares, keep an Amethyst under your pillow to ensure pleasant dreams.

- **Bloodstone** is the stone to use if your insomnia is caused by negative environmental influences such as pylons, mobile phone masts or disturbed earth energies. It works best if placed in a bowl of water by your bed. Remember to change the water regularly.

- **Sodalite** has a calming influence and this is the stone to use if night terrors, panic attacks, subconscious fears or internal conflict are affecting your mind. Not only does it help you to see where the conflicts lie, but it also assists you to understand fully the circumstances in which you find yourself, removing the underlying cause of the sleep disturbance.

CRYSTALS FOR CLEARING AND PROTECTION

If you feel drawn to wear a particular crystal, it may well be because you are subconsciously registering a need for its protective vibes. Crystal vibrations are excellent for counteracting negative energy of all kinds: gently deflecting negative energy, they stabilize excess energy and absorb toxicity, creating harmony within your home, workplace or external surroundings.

CRYSTAL PROTECTION

Several of the crystals in your crystal toolkit are extremely efficient at protecting against ill-wishing (someone wishing you ill) or energy leaching (the draining of energy), and many will transform other people's negative attitudes or emotions such as envy and jealousy that may adversely affect you. Sensitive people often experience a pull in their solar plexus if anyone is drawing on their energy. If you notice this, taping Yellow Jasper over your solar plexus helps to protects it. However, if you are the focus for ill-wishing, wear Amethyst or Labradorite around your neck to protect youself.

A Smoky Quartz crystal can be programmed and placed in your car to keep it, and you, safe at all times. Simply hold the crystal in your hands for a few moments, visualizing it surrounded by light, and ask that it will afford protection to you, your passengers and your car.

Green Aventurine

PROTECTING YOUR ENERGY

Energy vampirism happens when someone feeds off your energy. A subtle form of energy vampirism occurs through the spleen. If anyone is draining your energy or has overly strong ties to you, or if you feel tired or experience an ache beneath your left armpit when in contact with a particular person, Green Aventurine will protect your spleen and revitalize your energy. You can also use the spleen protection pyramid (below) to protect your energy.

THE SPLEEN PROTECTION PYRAMID

1. Sit comfortably. Using your *Green Aventurine*, trace a large triangle from just below your left armpit down towards your navel, then around your waist to the opposite point near your spine. Finally, bring the crystal back to your starting point (as shown). Visualize this triangle as a pyramid surrounding your spleen.

2. Now place your *Green Aventurine* about a hand's breadth beneath your armpit for about 20 minutes to heal and re-energize your spleen.

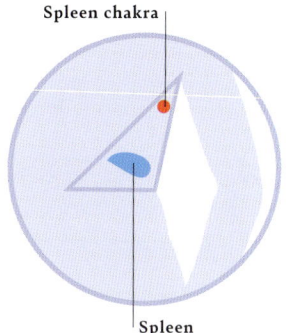

Spleen chakra

Spleen

PROTECTING YOUR HOME

Crystals are beautiful, decorative objects that can enhance your home, but they have a practical purpose too: they can keep the vibes harmonious and the energies vibrant. Crystals will protect against environmental pollution or electromagnetic smog (caused by the likes of microwaves, radio waves and radar radiation) – and against noisy neighbours. Remember to cleanse the crystals in your home regularly.

CRYSTALS TO PROTECT YOUR HOME

- **Amethyst** is one of the great protector stones, Amethyst brings a high spiritual vibration into your home. Guarding against psychic attack and ill-wishing, it also blocks geopathic stress and environmental pollution and transmutes negativity.

- **Bloodstone** usually works on the physical body, but its ability to block out undesirable influences also extends to the home. Place a Bloodstone at each corner of your house to keep you safe.

- **Orange Carnelian** kept close to the front door will attract an abundance of good things to your home.

Bloodstone

- **Rose Quartz** placed against a party wall ensures peace and tranquillity from your neighbours and brings harmony to both houses. It is particularly useful if you have noisy, inconsiderate neighbours as it quietens their emanations, promotes consideration for others and encourages them to turn the sound down. However, Rose Quartz can also create a beautiful environment in any home, clearing negative energy and replacing it with love.

- **Smoky Quartz** is a useful stone if your home is near an electricity pylon or phone mast. Smoky Quartz placed in the window nearest the source of such environmental smog, deflects the negative energy and also works for nuclear power or x-rays. If the energies in your home have become polluted in any way, such as having someone who has a negative attitude in the house or anyone who is putting out depressed vibes, then the Smoky Quartz will mop up the negativity and replace it with brighter vibes.

Smoky Quartz

- **Sodalite** absorbs the emanations of high-frequency communication antennas, infrared, microwaves and radar. Sodalite also blocks out the subtle emanations from your home computer and is effective against other forms of electromagnetic smog. If your home has a great deal of static in it, place Sodalite in the room to absorb it. You can also wash down surfaces with Sodalite elixir or spray it around the room.

Sodalite

ENHANCING YOUR WORKSPACE

Crystals are discreet tools for enhancing your workspace and for encouraging co-operation between co-workers. You can use a crystal as a paperweight, slip one into a plant pot or place one on your computer. It is also beneficial to spritz the area with suitable gem elixirs. A small crystal can have just as powerful an effect as a large one. A small Orange Carnelian, for instance, energizes a whole room.

CRYSTALS AT WORK

- **Blue Lace Agate** quickly restores peace and harmony if there is discord within your working environment.

- **Green Aventurine** promotes empathic leadership and is highly effective for absorbing electromagnetic smog and environmental pollution and for creating prosperity. This crystal defuses negative situations and turns them around. Place one at each corner of your desk, or in the drawers, if you have a co-worker who leaches your energy.

- **Labradorite's** iridescent energy enhances group energy and improves co-operation among co-workers. It encourages acceptance of new ideas and the sharing of insights that will benefit the whole, creating a harmonious working environment.

- **Orange Carnelian's** vibrant energies keep your workspace as energetic as possible – not in a frenetic way, but rather in a manner which optimizes effort. This stone attracts abundant good fortune into your working life, helping you to achieve maximum success and get things done as quickly as possible.

Labradorite

- **Smoky Quartz** protects against other people's stress and frustration as well as blocking electromagnetic smog and geopathic stress, and quickly clears your workspace of negative vibes. It alleviates communication difficulties; keep one near your telephone and spray the room regularly to clear negativity.

- **Sodalite** sprayed around the building or placed in the four corners of your room neutralizes the effect of 'sick building syndrome'. Sick building syndrome is often linked to an hermetically sealed building that has no natural light or air and which suffers from electromagnetic pollution and static electricity. Sodalite also absorbs the emanations of fluorescent tubes and computers. This stone enhances the workings of a group, instilling a sense of trust and solidarity of purpose. It promotes good companionship and harmony between co-workers, and its ability to bring things into the open non-judgementally is useful if any kind of assessment or appraisal has to be carried out.

CRYSTALS AND ELECTRONICS

The subtle emanations from electrical equipment can seriously damage the biomagnetic sheath surrounding your body. Kirlian photography can take pictures of the energy around your body, and can demonstrate, for example, that the emanations from a mobile phone create gaps in the biomagnetic sheath around the head and neck, and also around the reproductive organs where the aura virtually disintegrates. This occurs when the phone is simply switched on; you do not have to be talking on it for the damage to be visible in your aura – or that of anyone who is standing near to you. Eventually, this damage appears as physical disturbances. (A laptop or tablet has the same effect.) However, help is at hand. Tape a Green Aventurine to your phone or computer to block the harmful emanations and restore your aura to good health.

Green Aventurine is an excellent stone for neutralizing all sources of electromagnetic pollution. It will block out the emanations from your computer, television or other electronic equipment. Sodalite and Smoky Quartz also block computer emanations. Place the stones on the equipment or wear one of them around your neck.

ABOVE (left to right) Amethyst, Bloodstone, Clear Quartz cluster, Green Aventurine, Red Jasper

ABOVE (left to right) Rose Quartz,
Smoky Quartz, Sodalite, Yellow Jasper

THE 12 CRYSTAL HEALERS

With just 12 stones in your crystal toolkit you can heal dis-ease at a physical, emotional, mental and spiritual level, or transform your environment. The stones in this directory bring together seven crystals for cleansing, energizing and activating the traditional seven chakras, together with five 'master healer' stones, for healing the body (Bloodstone), mind (Clear Quartz), emotions (Rose Quartz), spirit (Labradorite) and environment (Smoky Quartz). The master healers also work on higher chakras that are nowadays coming into play. However, all 12 specially selected stones are extremely versatile and will have a healing effect at all levels. They can also be combined together as shown in the earlier chapters.

Within this directory, the introduction to each stone briefly describes the effect of the crystal, and the chart indicates the organs, glands and systems of the body it applies to, along with a summary of its functions and the chakras with which it resonates. Further sections follow, showing its effect on your body, emotions, mind, spirit and the environment, and describing the most beneficial placement. To select a stone for use, read through all the introductions. As the condition for which you seek healing is unlikely to exist at only one level, and will undoubtedly have contributory factors, two or three stones are likely to stand out above the others as being appropriate for you. Check these out in more detail until you pinpoint exactly the stone for your needs. Then all you have to decide is whether to use the stone itself or to prepare a gem elixir as shown on page 13.

If long-term wear is recommended, you can place your stone in a metal spiral and wear this around your neck – over the thymus gland about a hand's breadth below your collarbones is an ideal place, or you can tape the stone over the organ or body part concerned – tumbled stones have no rough edges and are comfortable against your skin. If you are placing the stones on any part of your body for a shorter time, it is usually sufficient just to lie still. Most stones work through your clothes although there are occasions when the stone is more effective against your skin.

QUICK REFERENCE TO THE 12 CRYSTAL HEALERS

Bloodstone
(see pages 70–73)

Smoky Quartz
(see pages 74–77)

Red Jasper
(see pages 78–81)

Orange Carnelian
(see pages 82–85)

Yellow Jasper
(see pages 86–89)

Green Aventurine
(see pages 90–93)

Rose Quartz
(see pages 94–97)

Blue Lace Agate
(see pages 98–101)

Sodalite
(see pages 102–05)

Amethyst
(see pages 106–09)

Clear Quartz
(see pages 110–13)

Labradorite
(see pages 114–17)

BLOODSTONE

Bloodstone (also known as Heliotrope) is a master healer for the body, focussing your attention into the physical realm and on to your life path. Radiating energy that can be used to balance the subtle anatomy of the body, this opaque stone, which appears green in natural light, is shot through with jasper that glows blood red under artificial light. This combination of red and green makes Bloodstone an exceedingly useful healing stone, particularly for the blood and blood-rich organs. Its influence on the body is amphoteric, in other words it sedates or energizes according to the body's requirements.

Tumbled Bloodstone

HEALING INFLUENCES

ORGANS	Liver, intestines, kidneys, spleen, bladder
GLAND	Thymus
SYSTEMS	Immune, circulation, lymphatic, metabolic
FUNCTIONS	Cleansing, protecting, revitalizing – particularly of the blood
CHAKRAS	Stimulates heart and base; cleanses and realigns the lower chakras

Raw Bloodstone

EFFECT ON THE BODY

Bloodstone has a stimulating effect on the immune system, strengthening the body's defences against infections, viruses and bacteria, and relieving chronic conditions such as fatigue or myalgic encephalomyelitis (ME). It also balances an overactive immune system as occurs in auto-immune conditions such as rheumatoid arthritis, thyroiditis and lupus; and is an excellent all-round healer.

Placed over the thymus gland, just above the heart, Bloodstone activates the production of T-cells, the natural killer cells of the body that destroy invading organisms. It reduces the formation of pus.

Bloodstone is a powerful detoxifier. It cleanses the blood and lymph to remove waste products and toxins from the tissues and blood-rich organs. Bloodstone also neutralizes excess acid in your body arising from faulty diet, toxicity or heredity. Its cleansing effect extends to the liver, spleen and kidneys – the three main organs that eliminate poisons from the body. The benefit to health is increased vitality and resistance to disease.

Bloodstone's healing influence also extends to your ancestral line, helping to heal the potential for hereditary conditions carried by your subtle DNA.

EFFECT ON THE EMOTIONS

Bloodstone's major contribution to your emotional health is to instil courage and to teach you to recognize when it would be beneficial to undertake a strategic withdrawal from situations that would increase your stress levels if you remained in them. Encouraging you to live in the present moment, it helps you to move away from the past and the effect that your expectations and previous experience have on your emotional stability. Its calming effect reduces irritability, impatience and aggressiveness and it promotes selflessness and sharing with others.

EFFECT ON THE MIND

Bloodstone's revitalizing properties are an excellent tonic for an exhausted mind. It reduces mental confusion, imparts mental alertness and strengthens your ability to make decisions. This stone helps you to adjust your mindset to adapt to changing or altered circumstances, maintaining your mental stability. Keeping a Bloodstone in your pocket during examinations or other stressful situations assists in keeping your mind calm, and able to focus on solutions rather than the problem. This stone promotes idealism and is useful when your motivation is somewhat low.

Bloodstone can also be used to promote biofeedback in which the mind controls the body – particularly the autonomic nervous system – reducing high blood pressure and similar conditions. This stone gets to the root cause of deep-seated disease, particularly that caused by obsession or over-indulgence.

EFFECT ON THE SPIRIT

Bloodstone enhances your intuition and enables you to follow the voice of your spirit. It teaches you how to express your inner self through creativity and encourages you to incorporate spirituality into the everyday world.

EFFECT ON THE ENVIRONMENT

Bloodstone is an excellent grounding and protection stone. It draws off negative energy from your environment and creates a barrier against undesirable influences. Placed in a bowl of water beside your bed, Bloodstone overcomes the kind of insomnia that results from negative environmental influences such as geopathic or electromagnetic stress which leave you feeling a bit 'wired'.

USING BLOODSTONE

Wear your Bloodstone taped over your thymus gland to stimulate your immune system. Placed over the spleen it will purify your blood, and over the liver it promotes detoxification. Add a Bloodstone to your bath to promote good circulation and to assist with detoxification – adding a handful of rock salt enhances this effect.

Tumbled Bloodstone

Raw Bloodstone

SMOKY QUARTZ

Smoky Quartz is a master healer for the body, earth chakra and environment. One of the most efficient grounding stones, it has a powerfully protective function absorbing negative energy and environmental pollution. Strengthening the survival instinct, Smoky Quartz is an excellent antidote to stress, promoting equanimity, fortifying your resolve and assisting elimination on all levels. This stone helps you to leave behind what no longer serves you. A natural analgesic, Smoky Quartz absorbs pain and disharmony and, with its natural radiation, is an excellent healing tool for radiation-related illnesses.

Tumbled Smoky Quartz

HEALING INFLUENCES

ORGANS	Heart, muscles, nerves, back
GLAND	None
SYSTEMS	Reproductive, nervous
FUNCTIONS	Cleansing, protecting, grounding, pain relieving
CHAKRAS	Earth, base

Smoky Quartz point

EFFECT ON THE ENVIRONMENT

Smoky Quartz grounds spiritual energy into the earth, re-energizes the land and assists earth healing. It absorbs negative energy of any kind and can be used to detoxify the earth. This means that it can be placed where the earth has been polluted with chemicals or with factory waste, for example. Over time, it will gently neutralize the detrimental effects and help the land to become fertile once more.

This stone blocks the geopathic stress created by lines of dis-ease within the earth caused by underground water, 'black' ley lines, power lines, quarrying and the like. In exactly the same way as the physical body has lines, or meridians, along which energy flows, and chakras that mediate the distribution of energy, so the earth too has its meridians, chakras and subtle bodies. Smoky Quartz corrects the energy flow in the meridians of the earth and restores harmony to the grid that surrounds the planet and so assists the earth's immune system to function.

Smoky Quartz also absorbs electromagnetic smog, whether from power lines, computers, phone masts and so on, which can have a detrimental effect on health in sensitive people. The pollution from these sources is unseen but it radiates out through the environment.

EFFECT ON THE BODY

With links to the lower chakras, Smoky Quartz helps you to accept being in a physical body, dissolving ambivalence about incarnation. It also helps you to

**Tumbled
Smoky Quartz**

accept your sexuality, cleansing the base chakra so that passion can flow freely.

An effective pain reliever, Smoky Quartz also removes cramps and fortifies the nerves. It helps to strengthen the back and muscles, and assists the body to assimilate minerals and to regulate bodily fluids.

This stone draws negative energy from the body and replaces it with positive energy. In a healing crisis, where an illness worsens dramatically during treatment, several Smoky Quartz placed point out from the body lessens the crisis. It is extremely effective for healing ailments of the abdomen, hips and legs and also benefits the reproductive system, nerve tissue and the heart.

As this stone is naturally irradiated, it can be useful in treating radiation-related diseases or for supporting the body during chemotherapy. However, care should be taken to select a naturally irradiated stone rather than the black, artificially irradiated stones which have too powerful a radiation level.

EFFECT ON THE EMOTIONS

When in contact with negative emotional states, this stone neutralizes them. Smoky Quartz brings emotional tranquillity, which is particularly helpful

**Artificially irradiated
Smoky Quartz**

in cases of depression that have an emotional basis or which produces suicidal feelings. Giving you the equanimity to deal with difficult times, it assists in leaving behind anything that no longer serves you and will neutralize fear of failure.

EFFECT ON THE MIND

Dissolving negative states of mind, Smoky Quartz encourages positive, practical thought and induces clear insights. It supports concentration, resolves contradictions and overcomes communication difficulties. This stone facilitates moving between alpha and beta brain wave states and enhances meditation.

EFFECT ON THE SPIRIT

Promoting a concern for the planet and for humankind, Smoky Quartz turns your mind towards finding a solution to the ecological and energy crises that threaten the future of the Earth.

USING SMOKY QUARTZ

Wear your Smoky Quartz as a pendant for long periods of time to protect your energies. Place it under your pillow for restful sleep, or attach it to your phone to protect you from the caller's emanations. Placed over a painful spot, it dissolves pain. If your Smoky Quartz has a point, place it point out to draw off negative energy and point in to energize.

Smoky Quartz pillar

RED JASPER

Bringing wholeness, Jasper is known as 'the supreme nurturer' and it reminds people to help each other. Red Jasper is a particularly sustaining and supportive stone, providing a reservoir of energy to draw on. It promotes tranquillity during stressful periods and brings unity to all aspects of life, and is helpful in rectifying unjust situations. It creates a protective bubble in which to journey or to undertake spiritual work, harmonizing all the subtle bodies that comprise the biomagnetic sheath, aligning them with the physical body and the chakra system. This stone supports dowsing and shamanic work.

**Tumbled
Red Jasper**

HEALING INFLUENCES

ORGANS	Liver, bile duct, testicles, ovaries
GLAND	None
SYSTEMS	Circulatory, reproductive
FUNCTIONS	Energizing, stimulating, grounding, rectifying, protecting, balances mineral content of the body
CHAKRAS	Solar plexus, sacral, base; aligns all

Raw Red Jasper

EFFECT ON THE BODY

Red Jasper is a protective stone that prevents absorption of negative energy either from the environment around you or from other people. This stone balances the yin and yang energies within the physical body to keep you healthy.

Despite its energizing colour, Red Jasper works slowly and does not over-stimulate the body, so it makes a very effective gem elixir or healing stone. In its capacity as the supreme nurturer, Jasper supports the reproductive system and the sexual organs, imparting vigour to a flagging libido and enhancing creativity on all levels, and helps to prolong sexual pleasure. Tape it over your base chakra to stimulate and open the sex centres of your body. This stone grounds energy and is helpful if you do not feel completely comfortable within your body.

Red Jasper has a strong affinity with the liver as it assists the detoxification process. It also dissolves blockages in the liver or bile ducts and strengthens and detoxifies the circulatory system and the blood.

If you suffer from a prolonged illness or have to be hospitalized, Red Jasper is an invaluable companion as it not only re-energizes your body but it also gives you courage in facing your difficulties.

EFFECT ON THE EMOTIONS

Red Jasper is a balancing stone with a dual action on the emotions. It calms when necessary and makes an excellent hand soother to play with during worrying times.

This nurturing stone provides a feeling of support and gives you something to lean on. But Jasper can also assist you in being more assertive when this would be beneficial to you. Keep your Red Jasper in your pocket if you have to face any form of conflict.

Polished Red Jasper

EFFECT ON THE MIND

If you need to think quickly and to organize, Red Jasper is the stone for you, especially if you require help in carrying projects through or putting your ideas into practice. Stimulating your imagination, this stone instils courage and determination, helping you to get to grips with your problems before they spiral out of control. It assists you to be more assertive and to be honest with yourself. If you have to face necessary conflict, Red Jasper provides support during the process and helps you to cope no matter what difficulties you face.

Placed under the pillow at night, this stone helps you to recall significant dreams, enabling your subconscious mind to communicate with your conscious mind.

Raw Red Jasper

EFFECT ON THE SPIRIT

Red Jasper cleanses and strengthens the aura and aligns the chakras, making it easier for your spirit to manifest itself on Earth. This stone has been used in shamanic work for eons of time. An extremely efficient protective amulet, it assists journeying out of the body and protects boundaries when journeying to other worlds. Hold it whenever you undertake spiritual work. Red Jasper also helps you to maintain your boundaries if other people are trying to influence you so that you can manifest more of your own authentic self on the earth plane.

EFFECT ON THE ENVIRONMENT

Red Jasper is an extremely protective stone. It has the ability to neutralize radiation and other forms of environmental and electromagnetic pollution. This crystal assists the environment by reminding people to help each other and work together for the common good.

USING RED JASPER

Place directly over the organ or chakra and leave for a prolonged period of time as Red Jasper works slowly but very effectively. It works best when placed directly onto the skin.

**Tumbled
Red Jasper**

ORANGE CARNELIAN

Packed with vitality and life force, Orange Carnelian is the great energizer. It is an excellent stone to use when you are feeling depleted and is particularly useful in old age. A stone that encourages creativity on all levels, this vigorous crystal attracts abundance and helps you to move into the right frame of mind to take control of your life through positive choices. It is extremely helpful in overcoming abuse of any kind as it grounds and anchors you into the present moment. Orange Carnelian resonates with the sacral chakra, the site of creativity and fertility.

Tumbled Orange Carnelian

HEALING INFLUENCES

ORGANS	Reproductive, kidneys, intestines
GLAND	Adrenal
SYSTEMS	Metabolic, reproductive
FUNCTIONS	Energizing, stimulating, cleansing, stabilizing, grounding into the present moment, bringing in abundance
CHAKRAS	Base, sacral and spleen

Tumbled Orange Carnelian

EFFECT ON THE BODY

Orange Carnelian has a powerful grounding effect that anchors you into your body and heals physical abuse. It is an excellent stone for restoring vitality whenever you feel depleted and is helpful during convalescence.

Stimulating the metabolism, Orange Carnelian fine-tunes your physical body. This stone is linked to the sacral and base chakras and to the reproductive organs. It is helpful in cases of infertility and low sperm count but also heightens libido and makes you more interested in sexual activity generally. Placed over the lower chakras for 20 minutes twice daily, it can be used to overcome frigidity and impotence. However, this is a stone for inducing creativity on all levels, not just the biological.

Placed over the site of the problem, Orange Carnelian is a useful stone for healing lower-back problems but it can also assist painful conditions such as rheumatism, arthritis and neuralgia. This stone promotes the healing of bones and ligaments.

Orange Carnelian has a dual action on the blood. It ensures a good supply of blood to the organs and tissues but it can also staunch excessive bleeding. This stone improves the absorption of minerals and vitamins and regulates fluid in the body.

EFFECT ON THE EMOTIONS

In ancient times Carnelian accompanied the dead on their journey to the other world. This stone removes fear of death, gives you courage and promotes an acceptance of the cycles of life.

**Tumbled
Orange Carnelian**

Orange Carnelian is an energizing stone that dispels apathy and motivates you to find material success. It is helpful for lifting depression, particularly when this has an underlying cause of emotional, mental or physical abuse. Encouraging you to trust yourself and your own perceptions, it helps you to get to the bottom of what makes you tick, particularly if there is a psychosomatic basis to illness.

Carrying this stone protects you against rage, envy or resentment – your own or other people's. It is extremely effective in banishing negative emotional states and gently quietening anger, inducing love of life in their place.

EFFECT ON THE MIND

Carnelian is excellent for overcoming negative mental conditioning and mental lethargy. Attuning day dreamers into everyday reality, it encourages analytic abilities and helps to clarify your perceptions, sharpening your concentration.

EFFECT ON THE SPIRIT

Orange Carnelian is not a particularly spiritual stone – it resonates with the lower chakras – but nevertheless helps you to express your spirit and joie de vivre through your creativity in the physical realm. It is useful during meditation as it removes extraneous thoughts.

EFFECT ON THE ENVIRONMENT

Orange Carnelian is an excellent stone for energizing your environment and creating a 'can-do' atmosphere. Grid it around your office or workplace (that is, place in each corner of the room) to achieve success in your career, and carry one in your pocket when attending meetings as it will encourage all participants to get things done quickly. This stone is a powerful attractor of abundance at all levels.

Orange Carnelian has the ability to cleanse other crystals, but it will also protect against envy, rage or resentment in your immediate environment.

USING ORANGE CARNELIAN

An Orange Carnelian placed beside your front door invites abundance into your life and affords you protection. This stone is excellent for creating good vibrations. If your creativity or fertility needs stimulating, place it over the sacral chakra just below the navel. Orange Carnelian is traditionally used as a belt buckle or pendant, and is best used in contact with your skin.

Raw Carnelian

YELLOW JASPER

Like all Jaspers, Yellow Jasper is a supremely nurturing and supportive stone. It shares many attributes with Red Jasper and the main difference in its effect is in its colour and chakra connection. Yellow Jasper resonates with the solar plexus chakra, with its emotional connections, and with the mental level of existence – because yellow is the colour of the intellect. This stone has a very positive energy, making you feel physically livelier, and has a powerful protective and detoxification effect. It soothes the emotions and releases emotional blockages and removes old baggage from the solar plexus chakra.

**Tumbled
Yellow Jasper**

HEALING INFLUENCES

ORGANS	Stomach, large intestine, liver, medulla oblongata
GLANDS	Thymus, pancreas
SYSTEMS	Digestive, endocrine, emotional
FUNCTIONS	Detoxing, energizing, uplifting, sustaining
CHAKRAS	Solar plexus

EFFECT ON THE BODY

Yellow Jasper is a protective stone that prevents absorption of negative energy either from the environment around you or from other people. This stone balances the yin and yang energies within the physical body. Yellow Jasper is particularly effective in promoting tissue regeneration, especially within the endocrine system. It is helpful in stimulating the pancreas and the thymus. It can be placed over the site of pain and left there to absorb the pain until the discomfort ceases.

Yellow Jasper works slowly and does not over-stimulate the body, so it makes a very effective gem elixir or healing stone. Yellow Jasper is useful for supporting digestive processes and for treating stomach disorders.

Yellow Jasper is an invaluable companion if you suffer from a prolonged illness or have to be hospitalized, particularly if this has to do with emotional or mental disturbance, or with the effect of the mind on the body. It not only re-energizes your body but it also gives you courage and calmness in facing your difficulties.

EFFECT ON THE EMOTIONS

Yellow Jasper is a balancing stone that calms the emotions when necessary and makes an excellent hand soother to play with during emotionally stressful times. This nurturing stone provides a feeling of support and gives you something to lean on. Keep your Yellow Jasper in your pocket if you have to deal with emotional or mental anguish, or need to empathize with other people's feelings.

With its powerful connection to the solar plexus chakra and its detoxifying action, Yellow Jasper can help you to gently release the emotional angst and the baggage from the past that is often stored in this chakra.

EFFECT ON THE MIND

If you need to combine imagination with organization, Yellow Jasper is the stone for you, especially if you need help in carrying projects through or to put your ideas into practice. Stimulating your imagination, this stone, like Red Jasper, instils courage and determination, helping you to get to grips with your problems before they spiral out of control. It assists you to be honest with yourself in facing the source of your difficulties, supporting you in finding a positive coping strategy.

Yellow Jasper also helps you to maintain your boundaries if other people are trying to influence your thoughts, and to be healthily assertive.

Placed under the pillow at night, this stone facilitates recalling significant dreams, enabling your subconscious mind to communicate with your conscious mind.

**Tumbled
Yellow Jasper**

EFFECT ON THE SPIRIT

Yellow Jasper cleanses and strengthens the aura and aligns the chakras, making it easier for your spirit to manifest itself on Earth. It is particularly effective in harmonizing the emotional body with the spiritual. This stone has been used in shamanic work for eons of time. It assists recalling what occurs when journeying out of the body and protects boundaries when journeying to other worlds. Hold it whenever you undertake spiritual work.

EFFECT ON THE ENVIRONMENT

Yellow Jasper is an extremely protective stone with the ability to neutralize radiation and other forms of environmental and electromagnetic pollution but is particularly helpful against petrochemical fumes. It also assists the environment by reminding people to help each other and work together for the common good.

USING YELLOW JASPER

Place Yellow Jasper on the skin directly over an organ or chakra and leave for a prolonged period of time; Yellow Jasper works slowly but very effectively. Carry your Yellow Jasper for protection while travelling or keep one in your car.

**Yellow Jasper
polished egg**

GREEN AVENTURINE

Green Aventurine is an excellent all-round healer, bringing in wellbeing and emotional calm, and is a particularly useful mental healer as it promotes tranquillity. Resonating with the heart chakra, this stone acts as a heart protector and heart healer, inducing a positive outlook on life. But Aventurine's protective ability extends beyond the heart; it is an essential stone for neutralizing environmental pollution of all kinds and for minimizing the detrimental effects of cell phones and computers. In addition, Aventurine is an extremely positive stone of prosperity, attracting abundance and good fortune into your life.

Tumbled Green Aventurine

HEALING INFLUENCES

ORGANS	Heart, lungs, sinuses, eyes
GLANDS	Thymus, adrenal
SYSTEMS	Mental, nervous, muscular, urogenital, connective tissue
FUNCTIONS	Cleansing, activating, regulating, stabilizing, creating abundance
CHAKRAS	Heart

Raw Green Aventurine

EFFECT ON THE BODY

Green Aventurine promotes a feeling of physical wellbeing. This stone regulates growth from birth to age seven and has a particularly strong effect on the thymus, guarding the body against infection. It prevents the over-production of adrenaline when the body is under stress. Holding the stone can lessen the sensation of 'being wired' that excess adrenaline produces.

This stone has a stabilizing effect on blood pressure and stimulates the metabolism. It can help prevent arteriosclerosis and heart attacks by lowering cholesterol and encouraging regeneration of the heart. With its anti-inflammatory properties, it is helpful in cases of allergies and, used as an elixir, is beneficial for many skin conditions. It also soothes nausea.

Gentle Green Aventurine can be used to treat headache or migraine and to soothe tired eyes as it pulls pain out of the body. With its regulating and stabilizing effect, this crystal is helpful in cases of malignancy or tumour.

Green Aventurine is particularly useful in alleviating psychosomatic illnesses. It assists you to explore the emotional or mental reasons behind the illness, particularly where these are located in the past, and can also dissolve karmic illness carried forward from other lives.

EFFECT ON THE EMOTIONS

Exceptionally useful in promoting emotional recovery, Green Aventurine stabilizes the emotions and calms anger or irritation. With its strong connection to the heart chakra, it enables you to live in accordance with the desires of your own heart.

**Tumbled
Green Aventurine**

If you have been receiving emotions projected from someone else, Aventurine gently returns them to their source.

Green Aventurine promotes empathy, helping you to connect with other people's feelings, and inspires compassion. It is extremely beneficial in the psychotherapeutic process, especially when used as an elixir, by both the therapist and the patient, and can take you back into the emotional causes of dis-ease. It helps to guard against one person emotionally feeding off another.

Green Aventurine is particularly useful for alleviating deeply buried fears and anxiety, especially those that arise from the first seven years of life. This stone is helpful in cases of stammers and severe neuroses as it brings an understanding of what lies behind the conditions.

EFFECT ON THE MIND

Green Aventurine stabilizes the mind and heightens perception. It is a useful stone for stimulating creativity and for bringing about a positive attitude to life. Seeing alternative possibilities, it instils decisiveness and encourages perseverance. This stone brings out innate leadership qualities.

With its calm energy, Green Aventurine is particularly useful for treating phobias of all kinds but especially claustrophobia.

EFFECT ON THE SPIRIT

Green Aventurine is highly protective of the subtle bodies that house the spirit. With its strong links to compassion, it also assists spiritual growth through service to others.

EFFECT ON THE ENVIRONMENT

Green Aventurine is a useful protector against negative energy of all kinds. It can diffuse potentially stressful or harmful situations and turn them around and bring them back into control.

Gridded (that is, positioned) around the garden, this stone provides powerful protection from electromagnetic smog, geopathic stress and environmental pollution of all kinds. The exact positions for the stones are best dowsed for but it can be effective when placed at each corner of the garden, house or room. Green Aventurine is helpful when invoking assistance from devas (nature spirits).

Taped to a mobile phone or tablet, Green Aventurine cuts out harmful emanations that can destroy your biomagnetic sheath.

USING GREEN AVENTURINE

Placed over the heart, Green Aventurine works on the heart chakra and the emotions. Bathing in the elixir is also beneficial, particularly for neurological or muscular conditions. Place over the spleen to prevent leaching of energy (see page 61).

**Raw Green
Aventurine**

ROSE QUARTZ

Rose Quartz is a master healer for the heart and emotions. A stone of infinite peace and unconditional love, it purifies and opens your heart, teaching the true meaning of love and forgiveness. If you have loved and lost, Rose Quartz heals the grief. This receptive stone attracts love, and if your relationship is problematic, restores trust and harmony. An excellent stone for use during trauma or crisis, Rose Quartz is deeply soothing and assists with accepting necessary change. This beautiful stone helps you to appreciate the beauty all around you.

**Tumbled
Rose Quartz**

HEALING INFLUENCES

ORGANS	Heart, lungs, kidneys, genitals, liver
GLANDS	Thymus, adrenal
SYSTEMS	Circulatory, lymphatic
FUNCTIONS	Enhancing love, sedating, releasing, assimilating, forgiving, restoring the blood
CHAKRAS	Heart, higher heart

Raw Rose Quartz

EFFECT ON THE EMOTIONS

A master healer for the emotions, Rose Quartz opens and purifies the heart, gently drawing out pain, heartache and grief, and restoring emotional balance and a loving vibe. Promoting self-forgiveness and transmuting internalized pain, it removes the residue of past emotional trauma, releasing unexpressed emotions that may be causing dis-ease, and dissolves old emotional conditioning and outworn attitudes and beliefs. This stone is the antidote to deprivation of all kinds but especially of love.

If, in your deepest self, you do not believe you have the right to love and happiness, Rose Quartz clears that false belief. Teaching how to love yourself, it attracts love into your life. Holding your Rose Quartz supports affirmations and you can reprogramme beliefs by repeating the positive affirmation 'I am worthy of love, I welcome love into my life' several times daily.

Sleeping with Rose Quartz under your pillow or next to your bed attracts beneficial relationships and can bring your heart partner to you. Its effect in attracting love can be so powerful that it sometimes needs to be balanced with Amethyst as it is not always discriminating in its action.

Rose Quartz increases your ability to empathize. It restores confidence and negates any false pride you may have that is covering up a deeper sense of inadequacy.

EFFECT ON THE BODY

Rose Quartz is a powerful physical healer for the heart and circulatory system, removing impurities from the blood and bodily fluids. Releasing the

**Tumbled
Rose Quartz**

psychosomatic causes of disease, it allows the body to return to equilibrium and is particularly useful where emotional pain has blocked the heart and the arteries associated with it.

Placed over the thymus, Rose Quartz heals lung and chest problems. Over the adrenal glands, it alleviates the physical stress caused by over-production of adrenaline and supports the kidneys. As the ears are the end of the meridian carrying kidney energy through the body, Rose Quartz can also alleviate vertigo. This stone promotes fertility and its coolness soothes burns or blistering; bathing in the elixir is said to reduce wrinkles. It is helpful in cases of Parkinson's, Alzheimer's and senile dementia.

EFFECT ON THE MIND

Reassuring Rose Quartz induces mental clarity and deep calm, and is useful for mentally centring yourself. Holding the stone brings instant tranquillity to your mind. If grief has been getting in the way of your ability to think, Rose Quartz relieves this. This stone increases your ability to express yourself clearly and encourages creativity.

**Rose Quartz
pillar**

**Heart-shaped
polished Rose
Quartz**

EFFECT ON THE SPIRIT

Rose Quartz cleanses, purifies and re-energizes the chakras and the etheric body. Rose Quartz teaches that if you cannot love and accept yourself completely you will never be able to accept love from, or give love to, another person. This is the stone of forgiveness and grace, bringing unconditional love into your life. It helps you to recognize yourself as a divine, spiritual being and to reconnect to the love that emanates throughout the whole universe, bringing deep spiritual peace. It also helps you to love others and afford to them the same forgiveness.

EFFECT ON THE ENVIRONMENT

Rose Quartz draws off negative energy and protects against environmental pollution, especially that of radium, replacing it with loving vibes. It radiates peace out into the surrounding world and can be programmed to bring world peace and to send distant healing to anywhere where there has been trauma or crisis.

USING ROSE QUARTZ

Wear Rose Quartz over the heart or thymus for emotional balance and healing; place it by your bed or under the pillow to attract love. Place it in your bath or add several drops of the gem elixir to promote forgiveness and loving acceptance of your self.

A large chunk of Rose Quartz attracts love.

BLUE LACE AGATE

Blue Lace Agate is a nurturing stone with a soft and cooling energy and yet it is a powerful throat healer and cleanser. It is particularly beneficial for opening a blocked throat chakra and for promoting clear communication, especially of thoughts and feelings that have previously been held back. Neutralizing the heat found in fever, infection, inflammation and anger, this stone gently dissipates any build-up of energy and allows matters to rise slowly to the surface for release. Its serene energy promotes peace of mind, and wearing Blue Lace Agate uplifts the spirit. This stone can, during healing, focus and direct sound waves (those produced by the voice or by Tibetan bowls and the like) to the appropriate place.

Tumbled Blue Lace Agate

HEALING INFLUENCES

ORGANS	Pancreas, brain, throat
GLANDS	Thyroid, parathyroid
SYSTEMS	Lymphatic, skeletal, nervous
FUNCTIONS	Cooling, calming, opening, activating, nurturing
CHAKRAS	Throat

EFFECT ON THE BODY

Agate is a stable and grounding stone that brings about physical, emotional, mental and spiritual balance, so it works as a truly holistic healer.

Resonating with the throat chakra and communication, Blue Lace Agate is extremely beneficial for conditions that affect the throat, neck and shoulders. The gem elixir is an excellent gargle for sore throats or for bathing sore eyes.

Blue Lace Agate benefits the thyroid and parathyroid glands, helping to regulate secretions and their effect on the body. Taken as an elixir over a period of several weeks (see pages 13), Blue Lace Agate can help reduce brain fluid imbalances and hydrocephalus.

This stone resonates with the skeletal system and, placed over the site, can assist in the healing of bone fractures – and will also heal arthritis: the affected part can be bathed in the elixir or the stone taped into place, if convenient. It also assists blood to flow through the capillaries.

Blue Lace Agate helps to overcome tension in the neck and shoulders, particularly where these have become 'armoured' by psychosomatic causes. It also gently removes any feeling of suffocation in the chest, and the physical conditions that arise out of this such as asthma or emphysema.

**Raw Blue
Lace Agate**

EFFECT ON THE EMOTIONS

An excellent stone for emotional trauma, Blue Lace Agate instils an inner sense of safety and security and dissolves internal tension. This crystal helps you to accept how you feel about yourself, building your self-confidence. It is a powerful stone for overcoming emotional negativity and bitterness of the heart. Healing inner anger, it fosters love and encourages you to start again where necessary.

Blue Lace Agate's most beneficial action on the emotions is in enabling your feelings to be expressed and providing nurturing support while this is done. This stone gently opens up the throat chakra, allowing the release of thoughts and feelings that may well have been held in the body since childhood. Suppression of emotion usually arises out of a childhood fear of being judged, or of being thought 'bad' by the adults in the child's life, and Blue Lace Agate helps to heal this fear and to lessen any feelings of rejection left over from childhood. Placed over the heart, it heals any emotional distress you may be suffering that prevents the acceptance of love.

The cooling and calming effect of this peaceful stone is helpful in dissipating anger or rage, encouraging expressing these in a way that will be heard by the recipient without provoking anger in return.

Blue Lace Agate encourages men to accept their own sensitivity and to be vulnerable when expressing their feelings.

EFFECT ON THE MIND

Blue Lace Agate is a powerful soother for the mind. It induces tranquillity and inner peace, countering mental stress. However, Blue Lace Agate also promotes self-analysis and perception. It improves concentration and brings to your attention the underlying cause of any mental dis-ease you may be experiencing.

EFFECT ON THE SPIRIT

Blue Lace Agate links to an extremely high vibration and to universal consciousness with its awareness of the oneness of all life. It encourages assimilation of all your life experiences, leading to spiritual growth and inner centring. This spiritually uplifting stone assists in speaking one's own truth and communicating the highest of spiritual truths.

EFFECT ON THE ENVIRONMENT

Blue Lace Agate ensures harmony within the environment; its gentle energies send out a peaceful vibration to counteract stress of all kinds.

USING BLUE LACE AGATE

Place Blue Lace Agate as appropriate, or wear it over the throat to enhance communication or to heal throat conditions.

Tumbled Blue Lace Agate

SODALITE

Sodalite eliminates confusion, enabling you to find your inner truth and assess that against the truth as others perceive it. It is a powerful mental healer that unites logic with intuition to increase spiritual perception and initiate higher awareness. Opening the third eye, it steps information from the higher mind down through the brain and into the physical level of being. Sodalite helps you to release yourself from rigid thought patterns and mental conditioning, and is particularly useful in overcoming phobias and panic attacks.

Tumbled Sodalite

HEALING INFLUENCES

ORGANS	Vocal cords, larynx
GLANDS	Pineal, thyroid
SYSTEMS	Lymphatic, immune, metabolic
FUNCTIONS	Regulating fluids, cooling, stabilizing, releasing
CHAKRAS	Throat, brow

Polished Sodalite

EFFECT ON THE MIND

Sodalite is extremely beneficial to your mind and should accompany any seeker after truth. It releases you from mental bondage to a specific set of ideas or beliefs and encourages rational thought and objectivity combined with intuitive perception. Overcoming confusion, it helps to clarify perception on all levels and, during meditation, assists your mind to fully understand the circumstances in which you find yourself. This stone enhances visualization and mental exercises. Sodalite encourages the assimilation and utilization of new information and helps you to put fresh insights into practice.

This crystal brings to light and relieves subconscious fears that are affecting your mind. It also helps to balance the conscious and subconscious minds – which may at times have very different desires and agendas – a conflict that can bring about mental dis-ease and which may lead to physical illness. It is particularly helpful for verbalizing your feelings and sharing these with another person.

If you suffer from rigid thought patterns or ingrained mental conditioning, particularly those instilled in childhood, Sodalite will release these, allowing you to find a more flexible mind-set that is suited to your present level of understanding.

EFFECT ON THE BODY

Sodalite stimulates the pineal gland and helps to regulate the metabolism. It treats calcium deficiencies and boosts the immune system, promoting lymphatic cleansing and elimination of toxins from the lymph glands. Encouraging absorption of fluids in the body, Sodalite also benefits the digestive system. This stone will cool a fever and lower blood pressure, and Sodalite placed under the pillow prevents insomnia.

The deep blue of Sodalite resonates with the throat chakra and it treats sore throats or hoarseness, as well as strengthening the vocal cords and supporting the larynx.

Sodalite combats radiation damage and helps to ease lymphatic cancers as it reduces swelling.

EFFECT ON THE EMOTIONS

Calming the emotions and bringing about emotional balance, Sodalite removes fear and promotes courage and endurance. This stone brings repressed shadow qualities (such as jealousy or shame) to the surface for release without judgement. It is particularly useful for people who feel defensive all the time or who are oversensitive, and it is extremely beneficial for treating panic attacks and phobias. Enhancing self-esteem and self-acceptance, Sodalite allows you to release the control mechanisms that hold you back from being who you truly are, promoting emotional health and wellbeing.

EFFECT ON THE SPIRIT

Sodalite brings about the kind of emotional balance that facilitates spiritual growth. It encourages you to seek truth, and to balance your truth against that of other people, supporting you in standing up for your beliefs and remaining true to yourself. It instils idealism and opens intuitive perception of yourself as a spiritual being.

Raw Sodalite

EFFECT ON THE ENVIRONMENT

Sodalite is beneficial for group work as it creates harmony and instils a unity of purpose and common goals. Increasing trust and companionship between members of the group, it encourages interdependence and promotes working for the good of the whole. By attuning the group to universal laws, it encourages living more in harmony with nature and the environment.

Tumbled Sodalite

Sodalite is also useful for soaking up electromagnetic smog and is especially effective when placed on computers as it blocks their emanations. It can be helpful to people who are suffering from 'sick building syndrome' when the place in which they live or work adversely affects their state of health.

USING SODALITE

Wear Sodalite for long periods of time especially over the thymus or thyroid. Place over the third eye to promote intuition and over organs as required.

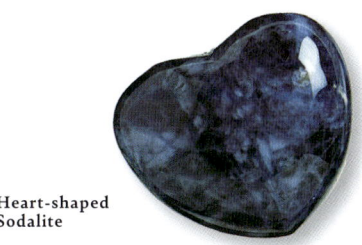

Heart-shaped Sodalite

AMETHYST

Amethyst is a healer par excellence for the emotions and the spirit. Activating the crown chakra and opening the intuition, it focuses your attention into higher realms. A transmuter of emotions and a protective stone in the physical realm, this transparent crystal, which ranges from the lightest lilac to the deepest purple, has a pronounced point in its natural form which can be used to draw in or draw off energy. An excellent cleanser and harmonizer for the biomagnetic sheath surrounding the physical body, Amethyst is an efficient pain reliever that transforms blockages at any level.

Tumbled Amethyst

HEALING INFLUENCES

ORGANS	Lungs, intestines, brain
GLAND	Pineal
SYSTEMS	Endocrine, digestive, metabolic, nervous, immune, skeletal, digestive, subtle bodies
FUNCTIONS	Cleansing, protecting, stabilizing, tranquillizing, transmuting, opening
CHAKRAS	Brow, throat and crown; balances all subtle bodies and chakras

Amethyst ball

EFFECT ON THE BODY

Amethyst has strong healing powers and is particularly effective in providing pain relief. Placed over the site of the pain, it gently draws it out of the body and in the process releases energy that has become stuck. For this reason, it is helpful in headaches and migraine, especially where these are caused by tension or stress.

As it fine-tunes both the metabolic and the endocrine systems, Amethyst boosts and regulates the production of hormones. It can be beneficial in menopause for calming hot flushes arising from an excess of oestrogen.

Placed over the site of a bruise or swelling, Amethyst quickly reduces these; it also cools inflammation or burns, and assists cellular and skin conditions. This stone also heals the lungs and the respiratory system. With its ability to promote beneficial intestinal flora and to eliminate parasites, Amethyst also benefits the digestive tract, particularly as it encourages re-absorption of water.

Amethyst has long been known for its ability to overcome addictions of all kinds. This is particularly useful when such addictions are having a detrimental effect on the body. Amethyst, used in conjunction with Bloodstone, can support during the detoxification process.

EFFECT ON THE EMOTIONS

A calming and soothing stone, Amethyst has a balancing effect on the emotions, smoothing out highs and lows and bringing about emotional centring. Believed in ancient times to ward off drunkenness, it is used to treat addictions and addictive personality traits – as these inevitably have an emotional basis – and it

**Amethyst
point**

can assist in understanding the root cause of over-indulgence of all kinds. It is an effective dispeller of fear, rage and anxiety; it also alleviates grief and sadness. This stone is extremely beneficial when there is a need to come to terms with loss.

EFFECT ON THE MIND

Amethyst is a natural tranquillizer and is highly effective at calming the mind, although it can stimulate this where appropriate. This stone assists the mind to focus and assimilate new information, quietening a scattered mind. It improves memory and concentration by facilitating the transmission of neural signals through the brain. This crystal is useful for insomnia caused by an overactive mind, and placed under the pillow it protects against recurrent nightmares. Amethyst is an effective healer of psychiatric conditions such as addictions or depression and a stabilizer of moods, but should not be used in cases of paranoia or schizophrenia.

EFFECT ON THE SPIRIT

Amethyst is an extremely spiritual and intuitive stone that encourages opening of the brow (third eye) and crown chakras. It has been used for eons to scry, see into the past or the future, and can facilitate out-of-body experiences. Enhancing spiritual awareness and connecting to divine love, it promotes psychic vision and entry into the higher realms. Tranquil Amethyst is useful

**Amethyst
cluster**

during meditation as it calms and focuses the mind and enhances awareness. It assists in understanding dreams and facilitates visualization so that the spirit can communicate with the mind.

EFFECT ON THE ENVIRONMENT

With its high spiritual vibration and serene presence, Amethyst has a powerful cleansing and protective function. Blocking out unwanted energies of all kinds, it acts against geopathic or electromagnetic stress and ill-wishing from other people, transmuting the energy into love. If you want to lighten the energy in a room, a large Amethyst cluster cleanses the environment of blocked or negative energy, while an Amethyst geode conserves and consolidates energy.

USING AMETHYST

Placed at the brow or crown chakra, Amethyst works on the spiritual body. Worn around the neck, it tranquillizes the mind and emotions, and placed over the site of dis-ease or pain, it heals it.

Amethyst geode

CLEAR QUARTZ

Containing the full spectrum of visible light, Clear Quartz is the master healer for the mind and the higher crown chakras. It is a truly holistic healer, uniting the physical body with the mind, emotions and spirit. Bringing harmony to the entire system, Clear Quartz is the most powerful of the master healing stones as it works on so many levels. This vibrational healer is an exceptional conductor and amplifier of energy, and simply holding a Quartz crystal doubles the biomagnetic sheath. This crystal attunes itself to your unique needs and adjusts its healing energy accordingly. It takes your energy back to its most perfect state in order to restore balance on all levels. The most programmable crystal, Clear Quartz can be used to cleanse, purify and energize all systems of the body, and is a deep soul cleanser and activator.

Tumbled Clear Quartz

HEALING INFLUENCES

ORGANS	All
GLAND	Pituitary, pineal
SYSTEMS	Immune, biomagnetic sheath
FUNCTIONS	Absorbing, storing, purifying, balancing, releasing and regulating energy
CHAKRAS	Harmonizes all the chakras, aligns the subtle body, activates the higher crown

Clear Quartz point

EFFECT ON THE MIND

As Quartz amplifies energy, it has the ability to amplify your thoughts – positive or negative – and is a useful aid to programming in positive affirmations. Hold your Clear Quartz while reciting or writing your daily affirmations. Programming your crystal by holding it and concentrating on the benefit you wish to achieve through its use brings about positive solutions extremely quickly, as this is the most receptive stone for any kind of programming.

Clear Quartz's clarity pinpoints solutions to a difficult situation, and the purity of this stone unlocks memory and strengthens concentration.

Clear Quartz can be used to remove negative thought forms from the mind. Thought forms can be created by yourself or other people: they are like a holographic picture of a thought that lingers in the mind and can be destructive or undermining. Hold the stone to your forehead for a few minutes and ask that the negative thought be transferred to the stone and dissolved within it. When you feel a release of pressure from your mind, you will know that the thought form has been absorbed.

EFFECT ON THE BODY

The greatest gift Clear Quartz crystal offers in physical healing is in purifying and re-energizing. It is particularly useful because it reaches deep into the body to cleanse the internal organs and restore the normal energy flow. By bringing the subtle bodies back into balance and alignment, the physical body is healed

Clear Quartz cluster

and restored. This has a stimulating effect on the immune system, bringing increased resistance to stress and dis-ease of any kind and enabling the body to fight off infection.

Quartz harmonizes and regenerates the natural crystalline structures found in cell salts, lymph, fatty tissue and white blood cells, and is particularly beneficial to the stomach and intestinal tract and for increasing the secretions of the pituitary gland.

Quartz soothes burns and can help to reduce blistering and tissue damage.

EFFECT ON THE EMOTIONS

Clear Quartz restores emotional balance and brings serenity to the emotions. When placed on the solar plexus, Clear Quartz draws off emotional turmoil and restores harmony between the emotional and physical body. Carrying a Clear Quartz can be useful in times of emotional stress as it not only promotes serenity but also gives additional energy to face the cause of the stress.

Raw Clear Quartz

Clear Quartz wand

EFFECT ON THE SPIRIT

This crystal raises energy to the highest possible level, enabling a very clear manifestation of spiritual energy and the reaching of 'altered states'. As it filters out distractions, it is an extremely useful crystal to hold during meditation.

Clear Quartz has the ability to dissolve the karmic seeds carried forward from previous lives and to take your energy back to the perfection of your spiritual self.

EFFECT ON THE ENVIRONMENT

Quartz can be used to purify and harmonize the environment, and a large Quartz cluster is particularly beneficial. If the points radiate in several directions, then energy will be radiated out to the environment. Quartz draws off negative energy of all kinds and neutralizes background radiation, including electromagnetic smog or petrochemical emanations. Attached to a fuel line, Clear Quartz conserves energy and reduces emissions, which has a beneficial effect on the environment as a whole.

USING CLEAR QUARTZ

Clear Quartz can be placed anywhere on the body. Add the crystal to the cold water and soak the burned area for at least 20 minutes, or place directly over the site of inflammation to soothe and heal.

LABRADORITE

A master healer for the spirit and bringer of light and initiation, Labradorite is a wonderfully mystical crystal as the unexpected flashes of brilliant blue from its greeny-grey depths indicate. A stone of initiation, Labradorite facilitates spiritual development by raising consciousness and dispelling illusions. It deflects unwanted energy from the biomagnetic sheath, forming a barrier to negative thoughts; prevents energy leaching from the aura; and harmonizes all the subtle bodies with the physical body. This crystal unites logic and insight and eliminates mental confusion. It has a powerful effect on group work and can act as a witness (that is, on behalf of the patient) during radionic treatment.

Tumbled Labradorite

HEALING INFLUENCES

ORGANS	Eyes, brain, gall bladder, stomach, spleen, liver
GLANDS	Pineal, adrenal
SYSTEMS	Metabolism, endocrine
FUNCTIONS	Consciousness-raising, protecting and filtering, grounding spiritual energies into the physical body
CHAKRAS	Higher heart, higher crown

Polished Labradorite

EFFECT ON THE SPIRIT

A portal to another world, Labradorite initiates into the deepest mysteries of life and accesses esoteric knowledge, connecting with the highest of universal energies. A deeply intuitive crystal, Labradorite stimulates the development of your psychic gifts and teaches you the art of right timing. It can teach you to look into the future or the past and is an excellent companion for past life regression as it focuses on truth. One of its greatest benefits is in screening and separating your subtle energies from those of other people during healing or intuitive work.

One of the great stones of transformation, Labradorite prepares the body and soul for the ascension process, an inflow of spiritual energies which will raise the vibrations of the physical body to a much higher rate, bringing in what is known as 'the light body'.

This crystal can remove thought forms that have become lodged in your aura. These thought forms are usually created by other people's thoughts. However, if you continually have negative thoughts yourself and expect the worst you can create a negative thought form which will create subtle dis-ease that ultimately becomes physical. Labradorite also removes psychic debris from your biomagnetic sheath which, if not removed, would create psychosomatic disease.

EFFECT ON THE BODY

Labradorite is primarily a stone for the spirit, but it also assists the body by deflecting negative energy that would otherwise lodge in the biomagnetic sheath and cause dis-ease. It also prevents energy leakage and aligns the subtle bodies

Raw Labradorite

with the physical, bringing about a state of harmony. Acting as a 'witness' during dowsing or radionic treatment, Labradorite pinpoints the cause of disease.

Labradorite is also useful for relieving stress and regulating the metabolism. It treats disorders of the brain and the eyes, and can be helpful in cases of gout or rheumatism. Lowering blood pressure, Labradorite is also an effective reliever of premenstrual tension.

EFFECT ON THE EMOTIONS

Labradorite is a useful companion during periods of emotional stress or change. Banishing fear and insecurity, it strengthens your faith in yourself and your trust in the universe. It is particularly helpful in removing the effect of past disappointments, but it can disperse emotional debris of any kind.

EFFECT ON THE MIND

Labradorite calms an overactive mind and opens the imagination. It helps to balance the rational mind with intuitive wisdom, encouraging contemplation and introspection. In this role, it dispels illusions and shows you the real intention

Tumbled Labradorite

behind thoughts and actions. It is particularly helpful in releasing reactive depression which, as its name suggests, arises from your reaction to life events.

If you are holding suppressed memories from the past, Labradorite will gently release them along with any other psychological debris that could affect your health. If you are ensnared in other people's mental projections or expectations, this beautiful crystal will gently disentangle you and set you free to be yourself.

EFFECT ON THE ENVIRONMENT

The scintillating light of Labradorite uplifts the environment and invites in a very high vibration from the spiritual realm. Labradorite's most beneficial effect is that of filtering out negative thoughts and energies, especially those of materialistic people. A large chunk of Labradorite placed in the environment will cleanse and purify energies, attracting guides and guardian angels.

USING LABRADORITE

Wearing a Labradorite around your neck ensures that your aura will always be protected and that the energies that reach you from the environment will be filtered and cleansed. It also ensures that your intuition is working well and that you will be alert to signals from your unconscious mind or from the universe.

Labradorite pyramid

CRYSTALS FOR SPECIFIC AILMENTS

	Amethyst	Sodalite	Blue Lace Agate	Green Aventurine	Yellow Jasper	Orange Carnelian	Red Jasper	Bloodstone	Clear Quartz	Rose Quartz	Labradorite	Smoky Quartz
Acid, excess								♦				
Addictions		♦[1]										
Adrenaline, excess									♦			
Allergies				♦								
Alzheimer's										♦		
Arteriosclerosis				♦								
Arthritis			♦			♦						
Bacterial infections								♦[2]				
Bile duct blockages						♦						
Bladder problems								♦				
Bleeding						♦						
Blistering	♦									♦		
Blood pressure, high		♦		♦				♦			♦	
Blood pressure, low										♦		

1 preserve elixir with
   cider vinegar
2 over thymus
3 in cold water
4 bathe with elixir
   without brandy

	Amethyst	Sodalite	Blue Lace Agate	Green Aventurine	Yellow Jasper	Orange Carnelian	Red Jasper	Bloodstone	Clear Quartz	Rose Quartz	Labradorite	Smoky Quartz
Blood problems						♦	♦	♦				
Bones, problems or fractures						♦						
Bruises	♦											
Burns	♦								♦	♦[3]		
Calcium deficiency		♦										
Chemotherapy, alleviate effects of												♦
Cholesterol, high				♦								
Circulation, poor							♦	♦				
Claustrophobia				♦								
Colds								♦[2]				
Cramp												♦
Depression	♦					♦						♦
Digestive problems		♦			♦							
Endocrine imbalance	♦											
Energy depletion						♦	♦					
Eye problems			♦	♦							♦	
Eyes, tired			♦[4]	♦							♦	
Fever		♦	♦									

	Amethyst	Sodalite	Blue Lace Agate	Green Aventurine	Yellow Jasper	Orange Carnelian	Red Jasper	Bloodstone	Clear Quartz	Rose Quartz	Labradorite	Smoky Quartz
Flu								♦[2]				
Fractures			♦			♦						
Frigidity						♦[5]						
Genitals										♦		
Gout											♦	
Headache	♦				♦[6]							
Heart attack					♦					♦		
Hoarseness		♦[7]										
Hormone imbalance	♦[8]											
Hot flushes	♦											
Hydrocephalus			♦[9]									
Immune system deficiencies			♦	♦				♦				
Impotence						♦[10]						

2 over thymus
5 over lower chakras
6 over pain
7 on throat chakra
8 over pituitary
9 elixir
10 on sacral chakra
11 lower chakras

	Amethyst	Sodalite	Blue Lace Agate	Green Aventurine	Yellow Jasper	Orange Carnelian	Red Jasper	Bloodstone	Clear Quartz	Rose Quartz	Labradorite	Smoky Quartz
Infection			◆[9]									
Infertility						◆[11]	◆[11]					
Inflammation			◆	◆		◆						
Insomnia	◆	◆						◆				
Intestinal disturbance									◆			
Intestinal parasites	◆[9]											
Karmic illness				◆								
Karmic seeds									◆			
Kidney problems										◆		
Libido, low						◆[11]	◆[11]					
Ligaments, torn						◆						
Liver problems								◆				
Liver toxicity							◆					
Lower-back problems						◆						
Lung problems	◆			◆						◆		
Lupus								◆[2]				
Lymphatic blockages		◆										
Lymphatic cancer		◆										

	Amethyst	Sodalite	Blue Lace Agate	Green Aventurine	Yellow Jasper	Orange Carnelian	Red Jasper	Bloodstone	Clear Quartz	Rose Quartz	Labradorite	Smoky Quartz
Malabsorption of vitamins and minerals						◆						
Menopause	◆											
Metabolic malfunction	◆					◆						
Migraine	◆[12]											
Myalgic encephalomyelitis (ME)								◆				
Neuralgia						◆						
Pain	◆				◆		◆					◆
Pancreatitis						◆						
Panic attacks		◆[13]										
Parkinson's disease										◆		
Phobias		◆										
Premenstrual tension											◆	
Radiation-related illness												◆
Reproductive organs						◆	◆			◆		

12 on base of skull
13 sip elixir
14 add to bath water
15 over thyroid

	Amethyst	Sodalite	Blue Lace Agate	Green Aventurine	Yellow Jasper	Orange Carnelian	Red Jasper	Bloodstone	Clear Quartz	Rose Quartz	Labradorite	Smoky Quartz
Rheumatism						♦					♦	
Rheumatoid arthritis								♦				
Senile dementia										♦		
Sick building syndrome		♦										
Sinusitis				♦								
Skin conditions	♦14											
Sore throat		♦	♦									
Stammer				♦								
Stiff neck			♦									
Stress	♦										♦	
Swelling	♦											
Thyroid problems		♦15	♦					♦				
Tissue degeneration					♦							
Tumour				♦								
Varicose veins								♦14				
Vertigo										♦		
Water retention						♦						
Wrinkles										♦		

CRYSTALS FOR THE ORGANS

	Amethyst	Sodalite	Blue Lace Agate	Green Aventurine	Yellow Jasper	Orange Carnelian	Red Jasper	Bloodstone	Clear Quartz	Rose Quartz	Labradorite	Smoky Quartz
Adrenals				◆							◆	
Bile duct							◆					
Bladder								◆				
Brain	◆		◆									
Eyes					◆						◆	
Gall bladder											◆	
Heart					◆					◆		◆
Intestines	◆					◆	◆	◆				
Kidneys						◆	◆	◆				
Larynx		◆										
Liver						◆	◆	◆		◆	◆	
Lungs	◆			◆						◆		
Pancreas			◆									
Reproductive							◆	◆		◆		
Sinuses				◆								
Spleen								◆			◆	
Stomach					◆						◆	

CRYSTALS FOR THE SYSTEMS

	Amethyst	Sodalite	Blue Lace Agate	Green Aventurine	Yellow Jasper	Orange Carnelian	Red Jasper	Bloodstone	Clear Quartz	Rose Quartz	Labradorite	Smoky Quartz
Circulation							♦	♦		♦		
Endocrine	♦				♦						♦	
Immune		♦		♦				♦	♦	♦		
Lymphatic		♦	♦					♦		♦		
Metabolic	♦	♦				♦		♦			♦	
Nervous			♦							♦		
Skeletal			♦									

INDEX

ACKNOWLEDGEMENTS

The Publisher would like to thank Earthworks and Mysteries for the kind loan of crystals for photography.

PICTURE ACKNOWLEDGEMENTS

Photography: Octopus Publishing Group

Additional picture credits:
iStock: Helin Loik-Tomson 12, JulyProkopiv 29, netrun78 4, 7, 59, tjasam 57

RESOURCES

Good-quality crystals can be obtained from www.exquisitecrystals.com (USA), www.crystalmaster.co.uk, or from Mysteries: www.mysteries.co.uk

OTHER BOOKS BY JUDY HALL

The Crystal Bible, Godsfield Press 2003

Good Vibrations, Archive Publishing 2006

New Crystals and Healing Stones, Godsfield Press 2006

Manifesting with Crystals, Godsfield Press 2022

Crystals for Beginners; A Card Deck, Godsfield Press 2022

Judy Hall's Crystal Companion, Godsfield Press 2024

Crystals & Love, Godsfield Press 2024